Reflections of
Rural Health
in
Piedmont North Carolina

Jean Dowdy

Marjorie Land

Glenda Hargraves

Reflections of
Rural Health
in
Piedmont North Carolina

Jean Dowdy

Marjorie Land

Glenda Hargraves

Triple J Publishing <> Sanford

Library of Congress Cataloging-in-Publication Data

Dowdy, Jean.
     Reflections of Rural Health in Piedmont North Carolina
Jean Dowdy

     1.   Medicine   2. Rural Health   3.   Family Nurse Practitioner
     I.   Title.

ISBN-13: 978-0-9840853-9-2
Cover photo by iStockphoto- sestevens

Published in the United States by Triple J Publishing, LLC

P.O. Box 1923 STE 119 Sanford, NC 27330
www.triplejp.com

Printed in the United States of America
Design by Triple J Graphics

Dedication

This book is dedicated to Paul O . Alston, the first Director of Orange Chatham Comprehensive Health Services/Piedmont Health Services.

ACKNOWLEDGMENTS

We gratefully acknowledge the contributions of those who participated in the early development of the program. This includes but is not limited to the following: JOCCA, schools of Public Health Nursing, Dentistry, Medicine, Pharmacy, Laboratory, Psychiatry and Nutrition.

Support staff including Clinic and Community Health Assistants, Clerical, Jantorial and Administrative staff. The patients who entrusted us with the opportunity to provide their healthcare.

A team led by Loretta Jean Dowdy, R.N. FNP, Glenda O. Hargraves, R.N., FNP and Marjorie G. Land, R.N. FNP compiled and put this information together.

*Original typing and organizational services were provided by Rhonda Dowdy-McComb and Shirley M. Harris, Director of Medical Records and Consultation Services. These reflections were submitted by the employees of the Health centers as they remember.

Mrs. Daisy Murray
Mr. Moses Carey,
Dr. Charles Campbell,
Mr. Wilbur Bryant,
Dr. Jeffrey Love
Dr. Theodore Brooks
Dr. Samuel Tipton
Dr. Jean Chapman
Mr. Steve Almond, Pharmacist
Ms. Sandra Hogan, R.N., FNP
Ms. Ruth Efird, R.N., FNP
Ms. Debra Freeman Brown, R.N. FNP
Ms. Jessie Goins Holmes, R.N., FNP
Ms. Marie Shirey, R.N., FNP
Mrs. Ophelia Livingston

Mrs. Julia Alston
Ms. Martha Lucille Holden,
Ms. Rebecca Thompson Clegg,
Ms. Alean Brooks
Ms. Helen S Farrar,
Ms. Barbara Eaves
Ms. Rosa Smith
Mr. Levander Smith
Ms. Edna Raines McNeil
Ms. Sandra Hart Void
Ms. Robena McCrimmon
Mrs. Faye Schulz
Piedmont Health Services Website

Counties Served: Alamance, Caswell, Chatham, Lee, Orange and Wake

Clinics: Chapel – Carrboro, Haywood-Moncure and Prospect Hil

Introduction
Piedmont Health Services

The story of the original Orange Chatham Comprehensive Health Services-now known as Piedmont Health Services calls to mind the above stated scripture as well as a spiritual that declares: "Look Where He Brought Me From". It is the story of the beginning of an unlikely addition to the existing Health Care System in North Carolina to the outpatient Community Health Care model of Family Doctors, Public Health Departments, Public and Private Clinics.

Health Care of quality has historically eluded many of the population that these clinics serve. This delivery system was a gleam of light in the lives of many persons who were falling through the cracks of the existing system due to lack of access funds to pay for access, lack of unreliable transportation and/or availability of services.

This program combined agencies of practicing health professionals, students in health professions (Medicine, Nursing, Social Work, Psychology, Health Education, Public Health, Dentistry, Nutrition, and others) in a collaborative effort to meet rural and suburban health care needs. The recording of the history of this program is of most importance. It documents this collaboration of many dedicated people who committed their time, expertise and who believed in what they were doing. These dedicated men and women believed that their service would make a difference and it did indeed.

We are grateful to those that contributed their memories of these early days and we admit that this task was made easier because of their contributions.

This effort does not represent a completed work but one that will continue to grow and make a difference as the program changes and adjusts to the Health Care needs of our people.

We express appreciation to our leader, Nurse Practitioner, Jean Dowdy for her unwavering drive to put this history to print. She was helped by many others who are also appreciated. Past and present members of this very special family are encouraged to add to this history, to correct an unintended errors or omissions. It is our hope and prayer that as this document grows and transitions, it will be recorded and held in the administrative office of the agency and in the public libraries of the participating counties and towns.

HISTORY OF ORANGE COMPREHENSIVE HEATH SERVICES, INC.

Orange Chatham Comprehensive Health Services (OCCHS), Inc. was organized on March 11, 1970. It was organized to provide comprehensive health services and education to all segments of the community, with special emphasis directed to that segment of the population now receiving inadequate health care and/or whose access to health care services has been restricted. The original funding for the agency was received from the Office of Economic Opportunity. The objectives of the organization under the auspices of the Office Economic Opportunity, (hereafter referred to as OEO), including health care delivery, community development, environmental health, social services, and other anti-poverty activities. Indigenous, non-professional individuals were selected in the community surrounding each health center provided with training to work to achieve the objectives of the organization. All of the corporation professional staff were employees of the University of North Carolina at Chapel Hill and were made available for provision of services for OCCHS by contract. These broad objectives were pursued under OEO auspices and funding until the mid-70's when the program was shifted to Health Education and Welfare, (hereafter referred to as HEW).

Under HEW sponsorship, the objectives of the program were narrowed to conform with the policies of the funding received at that time. The program began to relinquish all of its anti-poverty objectives and activities and to trim its staff to conform with the different standards inherent in the transition from OEO to HEW. This change required the program to transform its productivity standards and expectations as well as its perception of its role in the community. Most of the original staff of the program, who was working in the health service component, remained.

OCCHS operated under HEW auspices and funding for several years with a streamline set of goals and objectives and a narrowed staffing component which eliminated social services, community development and others. The program and its funding then switched to the Department of Health and Human Services. At the time of this change, only the health services component of the program remained. This change in funding necessitated further transformation of the organization's goals and objectives as well as the productivity and operating standards inherent in the organization. Most of the original staff hired by the agency remained at this point. The expectations of funding agencies has changed, the attitude expectation and performance standards of the organization for its staff had not completed the full transition inherent in the evolution of its funding sources. The program has yet to make the complete transition in its expectations for operating standards consistent with its current source of funding and up to date management principal. These include increased efficiency, improved productivity and quality of service and more integration into the total health system in the geographic area in which the program is located.

The original linkage with the Division of health Affairs at the University of North Carolina including the UNC Medical School, has provided a consistent means for relationships among health care providers to ensure the quality of care delivered in OCCHS clinics is maintained at a high level. Three of the pioneers in the evolution of the role of Family Nurse Practitioners were working in OCCHS clinics at the time they wrote the book which is currently being used as protocols for standing orders for the practice of Family Nurse Practitioners in many states. Two of these individuals have remained employed at OCCHS since the early 70's.

While the corporation no longer contracts with the University of North Carolina for professional staff (now employs its own) many of the original professionals who participated under the contract have remained with OCHHS since they began work with the University of North Carolina.

OCCHS has had only two Executive Directors in its 16 year history. Mr. Paul Alston, who helped initiate the program continued to provide leadership for it until early 1986. The current Project Director, Moses Carey, Jr., assumed the responsibility of this role on August 1, 1986.

OCCHS Demography and Geography

OCCHS currently operates three community health centers. These centers are located in Southeastern Caswell County at Prospect Hill, North Carolina, Carrboro, North Carolina in Orange County and in Southeastern Chatham County at Haywood-Moncure, North Carolina. Both Prospect Hill and Haywood-Moncure are highly rural areas with the nearest small town (town of at least 2,000 people) being 10 miles away. The Carrboro Center is located in a community which includes Chapel Hill, North Carolina in Southeastern Orange County. The towns of Chapel Hill and Carrboro include approximately 50,000 people. With a current population of approximately 83,170, Orange County is one of the fastest growing counties in North Carolina. The 1986 population represents a 48% increase in the population and is expected to be 100,605 (plus 17,435) a 21% increase above the 1986 population respectively. (See Appendix number one). Due to the impact of the Research Triangle Park area which is eight miles from Chapel Hill, most of the growth inherent in these figures, will occur in Orange County, in and around the Chapel Hill-Carrboro area. Similar growth patterns are expected in Northern Chatham County which is also in close proximity to Chapel Hill and the Research Triangle Park. These are areas served by both Chapel Hill-Carrboro Center and the Haywood-Moncure Center.

The service area of OCCHS includes parts of the second, fourth, and sixth congressional district. It also includes all or parts of five counties in North

Central North Carolina. These counties are: Orange, Chatham, Person, Caswell and Lee Counties. Within this and contiguous areas, OCCHS serves 45,222 registered patients. Of this number 24,929 are considered to be active patients (at least one visit to a health center within the last 24 months). These numbers are divided among the three health centers as shown in attachment number three. The economic picture of Orange County is rather skewed by the high education and income levels of individuals living in Southern Orange Counties who are employees of the University of North Carolina at Chapel Hill and/or the Research Triangle Park. While the absolute number of these individuals is increasing, their proportion in the overall population is not. This means that the number of individuals who are employed in the service industry and other under employed positions is also increasing. This is the group that is at or near the poverty level and which depend on the services provided by OCCHS in higher proportions than the general population. This group includes many University of North Carolina and other governmental employees who are included in the unskilled labor force. In addition, the area is experiencing an influx of individuals looking for employment due to the publicity received in National media sources, concerning the low unemployment rate and the rapid growth rate. The booming construction industry has caused an immigration of Spanish-speaking Americans who are employed in the construction industry. Many of these individuals complete the construction work they came to the area to find and stay on as permanent citizens in the area, working in service and unskilled related jobs. In the last year, two textile industry operations have discontinued business in Orange County. This has caused approximately 1200 individuals to become unemployed during that period of time. Most of these individuals live in Central and Northern Orange County which includes the service area of the Chapel Hill-Carrboro and the Prospect Hill Centers. This trend is expected to continue unless the national position on competition from foreign textile products is changed. Consequently, the number of medically indigent in the Chapel Hill and Prospect Hill service can increase substantially over night. This takes into consideration the families of those workers laid off due to plant closings.

Four Significant Leaders

Paul O. Alston

Moses Carey, Jr.

Glenn Pickard

Robert Lawrence

PAUL O. ALSTON

Biographical Data for Paul O. Alston

Personal:

Date of birth	November 22, 1924
Place of Birth	Siler City, North Carolina
Married to	Julia M. Bethea
	of Hamlet, North Carolina
Children	Mary Frances
	Paula Parrish

Education:

Bachelor of Science   Agricultural and Technical College
                             Greensboro, North Carolina 1951

Master of Science   Agricultural and Technical College
                             Greensboro, North Carolina 1955

National Science Foundation 1959, 1962, 1963

Further Studies:
           North Carolina Central University at Durham, North Carolina
           University of North Carolina at Chapel Hill, North Carolina
           United States Department of Health, Education and welfare
           Public Health Service, National center for Health Statistics
           Statistical Methods in Diagnosing Community Health Statistics
           Capabilities and Limitations of Computer Systems
           Statistical Methods In Public Health
           Family Planning Statistics

Completed Requirements for the Master Degree of Health Administration

1970 to Present	Project Director, Orange-Chatham Comprehensive Health Services
1967 to 1970	Executive Director, Joint Orange Chatham Community Action Agency
1952 to 1967	Guidance Counselor, Assistant to the Principal and Teacher
1946 to 1948	Foreman, U.S. Steel, Tonawanda, New York
1942 to1946	United States Army Air Force and 364thCombat Infantry 145 2nd Evacuation Command

Professional Affiliations:

Sigma Rho Sigma – National Honorary Society
National Geographic Society American Chemical Society

Paul O. Alston

In June 1980, Dr. Gary Lewis, President of the North Carolina Primary Health Care Association presented Paul Alston an award at the organization's annual meeting. He recognized Paul as having the strongest consumer oriented health care program in the state. He and his board have truly made Orange Chatham Comprehensive Health Services a comprehensive center at a time when many obstacles were hindering his progress. His major hindrance was that political administrations of this time did not favor programs that emphasized the poor. Another problem came from the location of one of the health centers which was in an area with four academic institutions and hospitals that saw the health centers as a duplication of their services and competition for getting funds from various sources. In spite of his many pressures, he never veered from his course or mission. It would have been easier for him to have given in to politics and bureaucratic pressures and to have forgotten or neglected the patients and communities that he served, Carrboro, Moncure, and Prospect Hill. These areas needed him the most. Instead he held fast to his objective providing quality health care to all people. Paul probably said it best when he talked about the philosophy of health care, "The patient comes first that is what quality health care is all about."

As recorded by Mrs. Julia Bethea Alston, a very supportive and
faithful spouse of Mr. Paul Alston

MOSES CAREY, JR.

Moses Carey, Jr.

An Administrator's View of the Evolution of OCCHS, Inc. to Piedmont Health Services, Inc. and its impact on access to primary care in North Carolina

My first contact with OCCHS was when I was offered a job at the UNC Division of Health Affairs in the Community Health Services Project, which administered the professional services contract that provided UNC health professional staff for OCCHS clinics. I was referred to talk with Glen Wilson, an Assistant Dean in the UNC School of Medicine by my friend Dr. John Hatch, who was one of the founders of the community health center movement in the US (a fact I was not aware of at the time). This was in 1972 upon my completion of a master's degree at the UNC School of Public Health where John Hatch and I were students. At that time, UNC Hospitals required physicians to be medical faculty members in order to receive hospital staff privileges, a system that for which only remnants remain. However, faculty membership provided instant credibility for professional staff from all health sciences schools who wanted to provide health care more than they wanted to teach. It also allowed OCCHS to recruit many outstanding health professionals. I jumped at the chance to work at UNC in the health care field I had chosen.

It was then that I met Paul Alston, OCCHS Program Director and Edwin (Ed) Caldwell, Assistant director at OCCHS. It was also then that I became acquainted with the outstanding class of Family Nurse Practitioners (FNPs) who were trained at UNC School of Medicine and Nursing and were subsequently hired by the Community health services Project to work in OCCHS clinics. The FNPs that I can remember from that class are Marjorie Land, Betty Compton, Glenda Hargraves, Jean Dowdy, Margaret Wilkman, and Hattie Nagle. I think there were only six in the first FNP class, all of whom were hired by OCCHS. I mention this group of FNPs because they were pioneers, along with OCCHS, in the early days of the mid-level practitioner movement, which was by no means widely accepted at that time Without OCCHS's willingness to hire these nurses after training, FNP program development would have been much slower. The only other midlevel program in North Carolina and perhaps the country at the time was the Physician's Assistant program in its infancy at Duke University, which trained former military Medics in primary care. I will mention other ways OCCHS has positively impacted the health care environment by developing cutting edge programs in the state and nationally since its inception.

While I met Paul Alston in 1972, it was clear that our visions for public health and primary care were similar. We worked together to move OCCHS and UNC toward their mutually compatible goals of improving access to primary health care in Central North Carolina. OCCHS operated three health centers at that time, which included Prospect Hill, Haywood-Moncure and the Chapel Hill Center. During that time I became acquainted with many dedicated staff that elected to work with OCCHS and would have done so regardless of whether they could hold faculty status. I worked with the university for three years as Administrative Director for the Community Health Services Program which provided professional staff to OCCHS before I transferred to the Area Health Education Centers (AHEC) program to broaden my professional experience. After leaving OCCHS I pursued legal training at NCCU, and was elected to the Orange County Commission in 1984 and served until 2008.

When I returned to OCCHS as Executive Director in 1986, it continued to operate the three centers which began in 1970 and 1971. Many of the early staff who were UNC faculty members in the early days continued to work for OCCHS, but now as direct employees. Some retained faculty appointments for personal and professional reasons. However, only those few physicians who retained UNC faculty appointments were eligible to serve OCCHS patients when they were hospitalized at UNC Hospitals (then known as NC Memorial

Hospital). The program had grown to serve more patients and the Latino population (about 5-10%) gravitated primarily to Prospect Hill Health Center. There were about 100 employees in all sites and the central office in 1986. The budget was about $3 million with at least 76 percent provided by federal grant funds. The remainder was received from private paying patients, Medicaid and Medicare payments. The physical facilities for each site, except the Carrboro Center and the collocated Central office (which had been moved to a modern building in Carrboro), consisted of temporary trailers that were put into use as early as 1972 when the program began. All were in poor condition and needed replacement for the staff and patients to have respect for the place they worked and sought health care.

The board of OCCHS was eager for new leadership with vision who shared the vision of Paul Alston to make OCCHS the best it could be while expanding access to care for all who needed it. I shared the vision and immediately set goals to improve/replace the building in which the Prospect Hill and Moncure Centers operated. This objective was impeded due to the almost total reliance on federal funds and increasing need to upgrade staff salaries to compete for the best staff. Therefore, plans were made to tap a variety of state and private foundation funds to help with both of these objectives. With technology changing fast, we also proceeded to improve our ability to tap insurance payments and clearly identify patients who were financially able to pay part of the cost of the services they received.

This effort resulted in tapping state funds through the North Carolina Office of Rural Health Services headed by Jim Bernstein (my friend from graduate school), Kate B. Reynolds Trust Fund, Federal grants through the Office of Health and Human Services, and a monumental local fundraising campaign by the Prospect Hill community to buy land and construct a new health center across the street from the original building constructed by the community to attract a private doctor in the early 1960's. The building was completed and occupied by 1990. The Moncure Center was the next to be constructed on its original site by 1995 using the same strategy of compiling a variety of federal, state and foundation funding sources to make it possible. This was a traumatic experience, though successful, because we continued to provide services in portions of the building as other sections were renovated. The results pleased many patients and staff.

During the roll-out of these construction projects I received a visit from Jim Bernstein and Maureen Darcy, a Nurse Midwife who operated a Nurse Midwife staffed birthing center in Siler City which had ceased operation because they could not obtain physician back-up, a legal and quality of care requirement for licensure of the site. They discussed the state of the market, the need for alternative birthing choices in the area and state, the potential for such services to help contribute to the payment for services to those who could not pay for primary care services, and the strength which OCCHS could provide to moving the Nurse Midwife staffed birthing center services movement forward in the state. After several meetings, they convinced me to ask the OCCHS board to pursue a joint venture with the UNC Family Medicine Department in a cutting edge project to change the way the prenatal and birthing services were provided in Central North Carolina and perhaps the state. The result was the opening and operation of a Nurse Midwife staffed birthing center that was well received by the women who wanted a choice of care. While the birthing center was later sold to Maureen Darcy who served as its director, and the women who worked there and continues to operate today, it did not reach the goal anticipated by the OCCHS board to attract enough paying birthing center patients to subsidize the care of primary care patients. Nevertheless, this is another example of the cutting edge impact OCCHS had on access to care in North Carolina. As a result of this OCCHS pioneering effort which proved that women across the state wanted an alternative to traditional in-hospital prenatal delivery and care, UNC and many other hospitals began to develop Nurse Midwife services within/or attached to their facilities to expand their scope of services. Thus they tapped into the demand for out of hospital prenatal care and delivery by Nurse Midwives, a previously undefined patient market.

The demand for services at Prospect Hill increased so much after the new building was opened that the waiting time for an appointment for existing patients grew to more than six (6) weeks, which could not be tolerated if quality and access to care were valued. Therefore, after analyzing the origins of most Prospect Hill patients, a plan was developed to see to provide services closer to the homes of these patients in Burlington to reduce pressure on Prospect hill for appointments. This plan resulted in a partnership between the Alamance Regional Hospital, OCCHS, the Office of Rural Health, the local medical society and other groups to open and operate a health center in Burlington in a building owned by Alamance Regional Hospital but scheduled to be demolished in a few years. This center was named for Dr. Charles Drew, the African-American doctor who invented the blood plasma separation process that helped save the lives of many soldiers. The objective was to try to correct the stories included in history books that Dr. Drew died after an auto accident in Alamance County because he was denied access to the local hospital due to his race. While locals, including the son of the doctor who treated Dr. Drew at the time if his death knew the true story (that he was not denied care at the hospital and was treated for his injuries), the myth was well established nationwide. Naming the center after Dr. Drew could at least stimulate a discussion that could lead to more people knowing the truth.

The Drew Center operated several years while a new building was planned and constructed in the East side of town nearer to its primary patient population. The Alamance Regional Hospital and many of the same partners who supported the initial opening also supported the construction and relocation.

By this time O.C.C.H.S. had changed its name to Piedmont Health Services,

Inc. to reflect the broader geographical area served as well as the need to reduce confusion associated with having the names of only two of the counties represented in the name when the program served all or parts of six counties at this time. It also helped in seeking private financial support from a larger area and group of potential supporters.

After developing credibility in Alamance County as a quality primary care provider Piedmont was approached to help preserve medical services in the Union Ridge community where Dr. San Scott practiced and was planning to retire, leaving the area without a doctor. Dr. Scott and his family of medical doctors and dentists had operated the Scott Clinic since the early part of the 20th Century. The board of Piedmont agreed to enter into a plan to purchase the Scott Clinic with the financial support of Alamance Regional Medical Center and others and employ Dr. Scott as he phased out his medical practice. The Scott Clinic was converted to a community health center and continues to operate as such today, preserving access to care in an isolated rural community and thus reducing transportation and other barriers to care.

While growing fast at this time, Piedmont did not shy away from opportunities to pursue Paul Alston's and now my vision of increasing access to care for needy populations. This presented the opportunity to apply for new federal funds to open a new health center in Siler City, NC where the Latino population was growing fast and many of these residents flooded the Moncure Center seeking care, Many did not speak English and needed translators to access care. The grant application was successful and with the support of the local medical society and hospital, North Carolina Office of Rural Health, Kate B. Reynolds Foundation and the Duke Endowment a new health center was opened in the basement of a local medical office building. Plans were immediately undertaken to raise money to build a new facility on the East side of town. This building was completed and continues to operate today with a majority of their patients speaking Spanish as their primary language. This adhering to the vision of improving access to care for populations in need living in Western Chatham and Eastern Randolph Counties.

While the rapid growth in patients served combined with the construction of all new facilities on land owned by Piedmont created financial and other stresses, the leadership would not rest until the corporate office was located in a permanent facility of its own which was not leased. The plans for this goal were completed in January 2005 when the new corporate office was occupied on land owned by Piedmont contiguous to the Carrboro Center in Carrboro, NC, which has been constructed there a few years earlier. By this time, all of Piedmont's centers (except Siler City, which was under construction) and the corporate office were operating in relatively new facilities which were owned by Piedmont.

By the time of my retirement from Piedmont in December 2004, the staff had grown to approximately 200 and the budget had increased to at least $12 million, which was supported by not more than 25 percent federal grant funds. The staff was the highest quality one could find and Piedmont was recognized as a leader in the community health center movement nationwide. Piedmont's pioneering spirit prompted it to expand services in underserved areas while prompting others to try serving previously underserved groups in current and new markets. That remains true today in 2010, 40 years after its origin.

As recorded by Moses Carey, Jr., Executive Director 1986 to 2004

Moses Carey, Jr.

Moses Carey is an excellent leader. He wanted the board of directors of Piedmont Health Services to grow with him. Whenever he saw an opportunity to provide healthcare to communities that needed it, he would use his creative skills to locate health care there. He was a fearless leader who knew how to work with the community leaders and governmental bodies necessary to increase and broaden health services. His political prowess was what Piedmont Health Services needed to expand and develop.

Mr. Carey could work well with people from diverse backgrounds to achieve the objectives of the organization. He was effective with local leaders as he was with state and national individuals and organizations.

The fact that Mr. Carey was an elected official was an asset to the organization. He knew how to network to get things done. Mr. Carey listened to people who did not agree with him on issues and plans and he says that the outcome was almost always better than the original plan.

As recorded by Mr. Wilbur Bryan

GLENN PICKARD

Glenn Pickard

Paul Alston was the director of the local CAP agency, oriented to community development in all of its aspects. He, as I understood it was a native of Chatham County and had many significant contacts in both Chatham and Orange County. As time moved on, OEO had moved into the health care arena, largely in the Northeast, Boston in particular. At that time, Congress had poured millions of dollars into these programs, and a strong Southern presence in the United States Senate began to agitate for programs in the South. Paul, in his position as the CAP agency director, received notice that there was funding for a community based health program in his area. He quickly made contact with the Medical School for he admitted he did not have the wherewithal to build a Medical Care program. His contacts in the medial school included Dr. Sheps-Vice Chancellor, Dr. Fordham-Dean, and Glenn Wilson-Associate Dean of Community Health. Glenn Wilson was also my boss. Eventually, Glenn Wilson was referred to me and my vision of a Nurse practitioner based network of community health centers resonated with his perception of the need and we began the long and often tortuous journey that created OCCHS. We had, at that time, made major efforts to open the clinic in Prospect Hill. Glenn Wilson agreed to do that if we would agree to develop a clinic in Chatham County which became the Moncure Clinic. This always struck me as a very fair plan, but the conflict about the Prospect Hill Clinic would never die.

I have only a vague and conflicting views of where Paul got his strength as a community organizer. I am certain there are people better able to comment on that than I am. He was always an enigma to me. Personally, we got along very well when dealing with issues one-on-one. In public, however, he frequently attacked me as the enemy. His relationship to the Medical School and the health program at OCCHS was always stormy. How the program survived to become the success that Piedmont Health is today is truly amazing.

As recorded by Glen Pickard

Bob Lawrence

Reflections on Orange Chatham Comprehensive Health Care Project

When I graduated from medical school in 1964, I planned a career in international health. It was also the time of the universal doctor draft, and I applied for a position with the Epidemic Intelligence Service at the CDC both to fulfill my service obligation as a commissioned officer in the US Public Health Service and to begin my work in international health. I was assigned to the Central America Malaria Research Station in San Salvador, El Salvador with duties as an epidemiologist tracking the efforts to control malaria from Guatemala to Panama. My wife Cynthia, our two-year old son, and I arrived in July 1967.

In 1968 we were shocked and saddened by the news of Martin Luther King's assassination and began to reconsider whether we should alter course and return to the U.S. to get involved in the unresolved problems of our own country rather than work overseas. Robert Kennedy's assassination a few months later confirmed our intention to return home to complete my final year of clinical training in internal medicine and to find a position in the growing network of community health centers funded by the Office of Economic Opportunity (OEO).

In 1969 we drove home from El Salvador to Boston, stopping en route for interviews at the Tufts-Delta Health Center in Mound Bayou, Mississippi, where Jack Geiger and John Hatch were introducing comprehensive primary care services to one of the poorest communities in the delta. Then on to Chapel Hill where my medical school classmate, David Ontjes, had joined the faculty of the School of Medicine and had alerted me to the discussions about plans for the Orange-Chatham Comprehensive Health Services (OCCHS) project. A third possibility awaited in Boston with a position at the Bunker Hill Health Center, affiliated with the Massachusetts General Hospital where I was headed to complete my residency.

In the spring of 1970 I made another trip to Chapel Hill. The dean of the medical school, Isaac (Ike) Taylor, enthusiastically told me that Franklin Williams would be returning from the University of Rochester to direct the clinical arm of OCCHS as the contract was being negotiated between the community board, a Community Action Program agency, (hereafter referred to as CAP), which had received the grant from OEO. I knew of Dr. Williams' reputation as a community health practitioner and researcher and was excited at the prospect of learning from him as a junior member of his team. I accepted the offer of a position at the School of Medicine with my clinical practice at OCCHS.

My wife and I and our three young children moved to Chapel Hill in July 1970, and I started to settle in as a new Assistant Professor of Medicine. Less than a month later I was asked to schedule a meeting with Dean Taylor. He greeted me with, "I have some bad news for you and some good news." Franklin Williams had decided to stay at the University of Rochester. What could be the good news, I thought. Ike Taylor then beamed his broad smile and said, "and you are going to be the director of professional services for Orange-Chatham!" I was floored. I had counted on the mentoring from Dr. Williams and knew that nothing in my training or experience to date had prepared me for the complexities of the first real engagement by the university with its community neighbors to address unmet health needs in the two counties. In addition was the preparation for the first nurse practitioner training program at the School of Nursing to prepare the frontline family nurse practitioners that were going to be the core of the clinical teams.

Dean Taylor went on to describe the administrative structure for the university's role in OCCHS – I would report to an advisory board made up of the five deans of medicine, nursing, public health, dentistry, and pharmacy; the chairs of the departments of medicine and pediatrics in the medical school and epidemiology in the school of public health; and presided over by the vice chancellor for health sciences. Ike assured me that he would "have my back" with this august group and went on to suggest that I start by getting to know John Cassel, chair of epidemiology.

Cassel was part of the "South Africa mafia," a group of five expatriates from South Africa who had been part of the pioneering community health center founded by Emily and Sidney Karks at Pholela in rural Natal province, what is now Kwazulu-Natal, South Africa. With the increasing repression of the apartheid government, the health center could no longer function as the multiracial program established by the Karks, the Karks emigrated to Israel, and five staff members emigrated to Chapel Hill. Pholela had already served as the template for early O.E.O. funded health centers in Boston, New York City, and Mound Bayou, and John Cassel knew all the details. A solid group of dedicated physicians – Jim Bryan, Glenn Pickard, and Sam Putnam – pitched in to help and were joined within a year or two by John Noble, Bob Greenberg, Ed Wagner, and Zell Hoole.

I plunged into a busy and stimulating professional life of seeing patients, teaching sessions for the nurse practitioners who would become my OCCHS colleagues on completion of their training, participating in the other duties of a new faculty member in medicine, and representing the university in negotiations with the community board and with Paul Alston, the project director.

Paul Alston and I had a complicated relationship. He was ten or fifteen years my senior, had grown up in Jim Crow North Carolina and attended segregated schools. I was, in his eyes, a bleeding heart white liberal from the North who couldn't begin to understand what his life had been like. Slowly we began to communicate. One memorable exchange occurred when I met with him to relay concerns of the clinical staff that the appointment systems were not working in the health centers, making it difficult to see patients on schedule and to smooth out their workloads. I expressed reservations about the methods of recruiting support staff and suggested that we needed to raise the standards of education and experience and to provide more rigorous in-service training. He slammed his hand down on the desk and said, "You just don't get it. You think this is a health program. Well, it's not, it's a jobs program and the sooner you understand that, the better we'll be able to work together." I was stunned, but as we continued to debate (argue would be the more honest word!), I began to understand his position. We eventually worked out a compromise that focused on more in-service training and closer supervision.

Paul and I often drove together to community meetings during the planning phases of health centers in Prospect Hill and Haywood-Moncure. One evening we were heading about 40 miles north of Chapel Hill to a community meeting in a grange hall. It would be the first time that blacks and whites had met together in this grange. I asked Paul what we should expect. He said, "It will be like a wedding." "Like a wedding?" I responded. "yeh," he said, "my folks are done with sitting in the back so they'll be on the groom's side and your folks (white people were always "your folks") will be on the bride's side." Sure enough, we walked into the grange, and the community participants had arranged themselves exactly as Paul had predicted. The meeting was productive with good exchange of ideas among blacks and whites and great enthusiasm for opening a health center in Prospect Hill.

On the drive back I asked more questions about race relations in Orange County (the schools in North Carolina had been integrated in 1968, just two years before OCCHS was established). Paul proceeded to tell me that in the North, whites did not mind how big blacks got so long as they didn't get too close while in the South whites did not mind how close blacks were so long as they didn't get too big. While this is an oversimplification of the legacy of racism and slavery in the U.S., it gave me important understanding of Paul's view of the world and of his view of me. We slowly made progress in working together.

I continued to push for expansion of clinical care and improvement in the management of the three health centers that had opened by 1972. Details of the contract between the local board of OCCHS and the university required ongoing negotiations, and I emerged more and more as the focal point for pent up resentments about the institutional arrogance of the university. Things finally came to a head at a board meeting when one of the board members said, "I think things would work better if we had a new director of professional services." This statement was promptly seconded and passed by the board. I had been publicly fired and felt defeated and humiliated.

The next day I reported the board's action to my boss, Cecil Sheps, Vice Chancellor for Health Sciences. He was furious, said the board had no say over whom the university named as director of professional services, and he would straighten things out. I said no, that the time for legalistic enforcement of the contract between OCCHS and the university was over, and that I had clearly spent down my professional capital and exhausted my effectiveness. I would remain as a clinician, but the university needed to appoint a new director. A little over a year later, Robert Ebert, my former chief of medicine when I was an intern at the Massachusetts General Hospital and in 1974 the dean of Harvard Medical School, called to invite me to become the founding director of the Division of Primary Care at my alma mater. With great reluctance my family and I left our good friends and community of Chapel Hill and returned to Boston. I directed the Division of Primary Care for 17 years, including the last eleven years as Chief of Medicine at Cambridge Hospital. My OCCHS experience proved invaluable, deepened my understanding of the social determinants of health, and profoundly influenced my thinking about social justice, and made me a better doctor, a more effective administrator, and a wiser teacher.

I did eventually return to my original passion for international health and served for four years as the Director of Health Sciences for the Rockefeller Foundation. I administered grants to projects in Africa, Asia, and Latin America and was inspired by the work of dedicated colleagues in countries around the world. But I also ended up living in airplanes. I missed caring for patients and teaching students. I missed colleagues in an academic environment. I missed doing hands-on work.

In 1995, I accepted the invitation to become the Associate Dean for Professional Education and Programs at the Johns Hopkins School of Hygiene and Public Health (now the Bloomberg School of Public Health), and served in that capacity until 2006. Since then I have been a fulltime member of the faculty in Environmental Health Sciences, Health Policy, and International Health. In 1996 I established the Center for a Livable Future focused on hunger, food security, and the food system. We now have thirty faculty and staff and support seventeen doctoral students conducting dissertation research on different aspects of the challenge of providing healthy and affordable food, especially to populations marginalized by poverty, race, ethnicity, or geography. Not a day goes by when I am not drawing upon the bedrock of experiences and lessons learned during my time with OCCHS.

Primary Care for Chapel Hill, Orange County, and Surrounding Areas

The initial policy at North Carolina Memorial Hospital at Chapel Hill, North Carolina precluded primary care activities by insisting that all patients seen have a referral from a primary care doctor from outside the hospital staff. Early on, it became apparent that many patients were receiving primary care despite this prohibition. Once in the system by a referral, they often were simply scheduled back for continuing care and/or referred to other clinics from within the hospital clinic system. Referrals often were nearly meaningless in that one frequently saw a prescription pad with the words "Dx and Rx", meaning "diagnose and treat". This was viewed as an adequate referral; however, it became clear that this was often just a "ticket" to get past the administrative barriers.

Obviously, one of the major incentives to becoming a hospital patient was economic. The hospital opened with an elaborate "means test", by which all patients were interviewed and assigned a pay category ranging from 0% pay to 100% pay. Patients were assigned to either the teaching clinic where they were seen by students and house staff, or to the private clinic where they were seen by faculty.

When the Division was established in 1965, one of the early tasks was to examine the failings of our Primary Care Residencies. One obvious flaw was the absence of "roll-models", faculty who were actually involved in Primary Care. An informal study revealed that many faculty actually were involved in Primary Care. This study simply was not acknowledged, formally identified, or well structured. These studies led to activities by Division members that led to the establishment of the first formal Primary Care Clinic, a small grant funded effort called "Continuing Care." Many of its patients were drawn from an earlier program, "Home Care", which had provided the opportunity for medical students in their senior year to follow a patient's home.

One of the central features of the Continuing Care Clinic was a clinic based Nurse Coordinator, who knew all the patients, and in the absence of the physician (who was often tied up in hospital or medical school cities), to provide care for the patient that quickly evolved to include activities usually not practiced by a clinic nurse. Clearly, this represented an institutional development of a practice long used in private practice—the office nurse as a "stand in" for the busy M.D.

Concurrent with this activity was an ongoing analysis by members of the Division as to the actual reasons we were failing to send medical doctors (MD's) into the small towns of North Carolina, the very act the medical school was chartered to accomplish. We concluded the following:

- It was not primarily a matter of inadequate or misguided educational programs. We continued to seek to improve in these areas, but concluded we would probably continue to fail for reasons beyond the medical school's control.

- The sociology of small rural towns was stacked against attracting MD's.

- The general migration of all bright young persons to urban America was in full swing. Bankers, merchants, other professional—all were leaving the small towns to settle in the rapidly expanding larger cities. Why should MD's do otherwise?

- The social amenities of the small towns were lacking—no golf courses, no yacht basins, no theatre, no concerts, etc.,

- The schools were generally not as good as urban schools, a major factor for MD's with school age children.

- The wives of MD's were often not from small towns and were very resistant to living there.

- Medical practice issues:

  o The salary and prestige of the small towns medical doctor (MD) had been eclipsed by the rise of the urban specialists. The small town MD got "no respect" and much less money.

  o The conditions of work were much more difficult. Most small town General Practitioners were in solo practice and on call 24 hours a day. In urban areas, the rise of small groups had led to call schedules of every third night or fourth night. Large multispecialty groups were uncommon.

The content of primary care practice was deemed dull and boring by those in practice. They rarely saw "good pathology", a recurring phrase of medical students who visited their practice. We did formal review of the literature and conducted several small studies of our own regarding this, and confirmed that a large percentage of patients seen in primary care MD's offices had problems that did not require the skill and knowledge of a physician. Problems such as routine physical exams, well baby checks, exams for marriage license, and other "form physicals" were actually the number one reason for seeing a primary care medical doctor. The list of common illnesses include the common cold, cystitis, high blood pressure, diet controlled diabetes, etc. None of these were deemed serious enough to require a medical doctor.

Our conclusion of this analysis was that we should quit worrying about small towns. If the citizens of the state were traveling to the nearby urban areas to shop, bank, recreate, etc., why should they not follow the same path for their medical care? The loud answer from the small communities and their elected political officials was that medical care was different. Most often this was cached in the imagery of an emergency that demanded a medical doctor in the small town. Careful analysis revealed this was seldom a matter of any medical importance, but it became clear we were not going to win this argument in the important political arena.

We therefore, began serious considerations of alternative health care delivery systems—a concept new to academia. Our experience with the Continuing Care Clinic and with the nurses in the local Health Departments had convinced us that nurses, particularly if they were given additional "medical training", could care for most of the common conditions seen in primary care. Furthermore, largely socioeconomic reasons, the nurses were still living in the small communities—often commuting to work in the nearby cities. The question came up, "why not formally train and deploy them to work in the small towns, backed up and "supervised" by the MD's in the larger towns?" Analysis of the care in the military where this function was largely carried out by corpsmen strengthened our idea.

Then, to our surprise, we discovered a working model of such a system—the Frontier Nursing Service in Hyden, Kentucky. A program there that had begun around the model of nurse midwifery had expanded and developed into a system of care for all conditions where the nurses (now called Nurse Practitioners) were developed in network of small community based clinics linked to the larger town of Hyden where there was a physician practice and later a small hospital. Largely funded by philanthropy, they had quietly been going about their business and developed the exact model we had in mind!

Negotiations with the schools of Nursing and Public Health led to the formal establishment of the Family Nurse Practitioner program with Dr. Pickard the "Medical Coordinator" for curriculum development and implantation as well as developing policy, admission criteria, etc., and also taking on the major task of selling the idea to organized nursing and medicine and the politicians. Soon, a formal program was in place. Experienced nurses from the communities to be served were recruited and enrolled in the program in Chapel Hill. Six months of combined didactic and clinical education was followed by six months of "internship" under the supervision of the physician who had agreed to sponsor the practice became the recognized program. The first class was held in the academic year 1969 - 1970.

Meanwhile, we were searching for a local community in which to demonstrate the model. We wanted a community with 30 miles or so of Chapel Hill that was typical of the small towns of North Carolina. After much discussion and negotiation, we agreed to open and staff a small clinic that had been built by the community in Prospect Hill, North Carolina, in an unsuccessful effort to recruit a physician. They were, at that point, quite frustrated and willing to try this as yet and innovative approach.

Our intention was to provide a demonstration model that would then become a teaching site for nurse practitioner and medical students. All this was done with the knowledge and somewhat reluctant support of the medical school faculty. Dr. Welt, Chairman of the Department of Medicine was quite candid—he acknowledged the need for primary care in small towns, admitted he had no knowledge about or interest in working on the problem, knew and, to some degree, trusted the members of the Division and therefore, supported our activities. Other key faculty probably felt the same.

During this same period, physicians at Duke, led by Dr. Eugene Stead, Chairman of the Department of Medicine, had been studying the same problems and had also concluded this was a proper role for nurses. An approach to the School of Nursing was rebuffed and Dr. Stead subsequently went to the military corpsman model and developed one of the first Physician Assistant programs. Initially, students were recruited from military corpsman who had left the service. Early on, students from other backgrounds were admitted and many other health science schools followed the lead and wide variety of programs developed.

At the national level, many activities were occurring addressing what had been formally recognized as *"the crisis in American Medicine"*. One such program was the development by the Office of Economic Opportunity, (hereafter referred to as OEO) also, known as the Kennedy-Johnson War on Poverty program. This program consisted of a series of neighborhood community health centers, largely in northeast and often linked to academic medical centers. Word came to the director of the local CAP program (an OEO funded economic development program), that federal funding was readily available for similar health programs in the south as a result of congressional pressure by then very powerful block of southern Democrats who wanted their share of the federal dollars. As we were moving to open the Prospect Hill clinic in 1969 - 1970, a delegation consisting of the local CAP program director and a representative of the County Health Department came to the medical school with the message that they had access to federal monies for a local health care program, but lacked the expertise and manpower to mount such a program. This delegation was referred to the *Division*, where working relationship developed that resulted in a partnering between the University and OEO to develop and operate a network of nurse practitioner manned community health centers backed up by the University hospital and its staff. Prospect Hill became a part of this network and opened its doors in 1971. This program has grown and developed in a close working relationship with the University and now operates five clinics under the name Piedmont Health Services. Other University sponsored health care programs have developed, but Piedmont Health Services was the pioneer outreach program from University of North Carolina at Chapel Hill.

Based on the success of Prospect Hill Clinic and the Nurse Practitioner program, members of the Division and other University officials were successful in establishing the North Carolina Office of Rural Health in Raleigh, North Carolina. This office took the lead in developing a series of similar nurse practitioner manned rural satellite clinics across the state. This program became a national and international model. Many delegations of health care providers and educators from the across the United States and several foreign countries came to visit and learn from the activities performed the North Carolina Office of Rural Health. These efforts were greatly facilitated by the political good fortune that evolved when it became apparent that the community leader from Prospect Hill who had initially invited us into this community was a longtime ally and colleague of the

William Kerr Scott family of nearby Alamance County included two governors, the longtime chair of North Carolina Senate Finance Committee, and a United States Senator. Such political connections were extremely helpful as the need for funds and the need to change the Medical Practice Act, the Nursing Practice Act, and the Pharmacy Practice Act to legitimize and legalize in the formal sense the Nurse Practitioner role and the system satellite clinics that developed.

These developments clearly emanated from the activities of the staff of the Division under the leadership of Dr. Berryhill. His name and influence served us well in our relationships with the community and the political structure. He personally had little direct involvement, but, in his usual manner, brought together bright, talented individuals that he trusted and then gave them the lead in developing programs of this type. Once committed to an idea, he was ever faithful and helpful as the political battles inside and outside the Medical Center waxed and waned.

Early Board Members

Emeritus Board Member

Mrs. Daisy Murray

Mr. Roy McAdoo
Mr. Benjamin Douglas
Mr. Mike Eyster
Dr. William Flash
Dr. Kempton Jones
Mr. Leroy Jones
Dr. William Joyner
Dr. Arden Miller
Mr. Andrew Murray
Mr. Henry Pleasant
Mr. Artemus Wilson

Prospect Hill After Control of Clinic

By David Kinney

Daily News Alamance Bureau

PROSPECT HILL - For 46 years Prospect Hill had its own doctor. To hear local people tell it, Robert Franklin Warren, M.D., was the best kind of country doctor, the ones who never knew that making house calls is now akin to violating the A.M.A. cannon. Anytime day or night you were apt to see Dr. Warren venturing forth from his house down to in the grove near the general store-post office, working himself to death trying to save lives. Like many of his kind, he ended up bolstering his strength with alcohol, staving off fatigue with a bottle.

"The folks knew he was drunk, but they said they'd rather have him drunk than most doctors sober," Jimmy Winslow recalls. "He was a pretty good old fellow." By the late 1950s, Dr. Warren knew he didn't have much time left and that when he was gone this little farming community perched on a ridge in the southeastern corner of Caswell County, would be without a physician. He got together with his cousin Joseph H. Warren, who served the county in both the state house and the senate, and they donated an acre of land as site for a medical clinic. But it would be more than a decade, long after both men's death, before Prospect Hill opened its clinic. And now, after four years of operations under the control of the U.S. Office of Economic Opportunity, the community is on the verge of regaining control over the facility it built.

Today, Prospect Hill Community Health Center is one of the best, if not the very best, rural health centers in North Carolina. Before it was opened in 1971, area residents had to travel about 15 miles to either Yanceyville, Roxboro, or Mebane to see a doctor. Now, the brick building the original Warren Memorial Clinic and three trailers offer a full range of medical service from X-rays to pediatrics to dental care.

There are 12,000 people living in the clinic's service area, and many of them use the facility. Most days 40 to 45 people receive medical care while another 15 to 20 get dental treatment. "A 70-patient day is not unusual," reported Jim Powell, the center's director. "We needed a doctor. You don't know how much that clinic has meant to Gilbert and me," Mrs. G.M. Pittard noted. "I think the community would do anything we can to keep it. We need it." Mrs. Pittard and her husband were among the people who worked hard to get the clinic. Dr. Robert Warren and his cousin, Joseph Warren started a non-profit corporation and began to drive to collect the $20,000 needed to build the facility.

Most of the money was raised and about $7,000 was borrowed to get construction under way. When the bank foreclosed on the loan, 10 citizens bought the note and kept trying to raise money to pay it off. The brick building was completed, but it soon became clear that it was easier to build a clinic than staff one.

The board of directors would bring a doctor up to see it, and he might be interested. But then the physician's wife would take one look at Caswell County's social scene and veto any plans of opening practice in Prospect Hill.

"It was especially frustrating because the longer we were without a doctor here, the more people began to believe there never would be one," recalled Geneva Warren, the state legislator's widow. And that made it hard for the directors to solicit funds to pay off the note. Nobody wants to spend hard-earned money on a dream.

The months became years and the years multiplied, but still the clinic remained empty. Finally, Mrs. Geneva Warren asked for one more chance. If it didn't pan out, the people holding the note could rent the building out as a barber shop, beauty parlor or whatever they wanted to try and regain their money.

She went to see Dr. Robert Warren's daughter, who was on the University of North Carolina's medical school staff, and was put in touch with important people there. Mrs. Warren also admits she didn't mind leaning on some of her late husband's political connection. This was in 1969 and plans were under way to operate the Prospect Hill facility as a satellite clinic of the medical school on a fee-for-service basis. That's when Orange-Chatham Comprehensive Health Services stepped in.

The OEO-funded program could offer more services and do more, according to Paul Alston, its director. And with its federal funding, it could. OCCHS had a contract with the medical school to furnish personnel to its clinics in Caswell County, Prospect Hill also became a site. In July, 1971, the clinic facility opened, staffed by nurse practitioners who were backed up by physicians. Drawing on OEO dollars and the large pool of medical talent at Chapel Hill which reportedly has more doctors than the entire state of Utah the clinic's programs expanded through the years.

The program outgrew the brick building, and three regular and one double-wide trailer were pressed into service. In addition to a full range of medical service, including a pharmacy, a County has but a single dentist. The federal grants also enable other programs, such as outreach workers to visit patients in their homes and a transportation project to pick them up and take them home, were started. On the surface, it would appear things were going fine. But late last year the community was given an ultimatum.

The rapport between the citizens and the clinic's staff has always been good, Mrs. Warren noted. In fact, the community had set them on a pedestal. And there had been problems, she had become so fed up with the management and mismanagement they gave us an alternative," she explained. "They said we will continue to serve you if you want us, but you must make a choice between us and the easy federal money."

Community leaders decided to stick with the current staff. They formed Prospect Hill Health Program, Inc., and elected a nine-member board of directors with Jimmy Winslow as its president. OCCHS didn't renew its lease, which expired on Jan. 1 and the program was given until April 1 to clear out. "The director of Orange-Chatham indicated he would strip us down to the brick walls," Mrs. Warren reported, noting that there were newspaper stories stating that the trailers would be taken to Hillsborough or Efland.

Geneva Warren and Jimmy Winslow went to Atlanta to pow-wow with U.S. Department of Health, Education and Welfare officials and see if she could be stopped. "It seemed like an insult to the taxpayers to move those trailers," she noted. After sending in an investigatory team, HEW officials told the new board it had to be under a federal grant, if it wanted to keep the trailers. Application was made to HEW's Rural Health Initiative program for funding. Now the community is waiting to hear whether the grant will be awarded, and OCCHS is still operating the clinic during the interim period. The April 1 deadline has been moved to June 30 of that year.

Mrs. Warren said the clinic hopefully will have the same staff under the new board, but that some OEO services, such as transportation project, will be curtailed.

PROSPECT HILL
COMMUNITY HEALTH CENTER

Prospect Hill, Once Doctorless, To Dedicate Clinic
As written by Herald Writer
By Jack Adams
Herald Staff Writer

PROSPECT HILL- In 1956, the late Dr. Robert F. Warren retired after practicing medicine for 46 years in the Prospect Hill community. There was no one to carry on, and few doctors wanted to move to Prospect Hill. "Every time we would just about get a doctor, his wife would decide she didn't want to live in Prospect Hill," says Mrs. Geneva Warren, whose late husband was a cousin of Dr. Warren.

The community decided to pool its resources and build a clinic. About $12,000 was collected, and a clinic was built. But, still,   no doctor! For eight years the clinic building was empty.

At one time, those who had led the R.F. Warren Memorial fund drive almost decided to toss in the towel. They considered selling the idle clinic building for a barber shop or store and returning the money to donors.

But help from the medical school at the University of North Carolina made it possible to provide part-time medical care through the clinic.

And in 1971, a federal grant from the U.S. Office of Economic Opportunity through Orange-Chatham Comprehensive Health Services gave birth to the program today. It is one of the nation's few Family Nurse Practitioner (FNP) programs. On Sunday, the community's FNP Program will be dedicated. An open will begin at 3:30 p.m. Eight people have been invited to make brief remarks during a dedication program at 4:30 p.m. They are former Gov. Bob Scott, Congressman Ike Andrews, Lt. Gov. Jim Hunt, Chapel Hill Mayor Howard Lee, former Congressman Nick Galifianakis and Jim Burnstein, representing Gov. Jim Holshouser.

Mrs. Warren said Prospect Hill has grown to accept the FNP program, and that it serves residents of Caswell, Person, Orange, and Alamance counties. There are four nurses on the staff of the clinic. In addition, three Doctors from N.C. Memorial Hospital at Chapel Hill provide services. The staff has six community workers – people who have received specialized training to help in medical care follow-ups. They visit patients at their homes, helping the patients to follow recommended treatment procedures.

The original clinic building is still used. But other facilities have been added, including a 24 by 50 examination unit, a dental unit, an administrative unit and an X-ray unit. People who go to the community clinic are charged in accordance with their ability to pay. A sliding scale fee is based on family income, number of dependents and other factors.

Mrs. Warren said people showing more confidence in the clinic.

She said this is due to the "high caliber of people" on the staff.

The clinic provides primary care only. If overnight treatment is needed, patients are taken to N. C. Memorial Hospital. A shuttle bus is operated by the clinic in case a patient cannot provide his own transportation. Mrs. Warren said one of the goals of the program is to form a local board. It is under the administration of the Orange-Chatham Comprehensive Health Services office now. A local board would not dictate policy or funding procedures, but would help develop more cooperation with the community, she said.

Jean Dowdy~Marjorie Land~Glenda Hargraves

Moncure
Community Health Center

History

Orange-Chatham Comprehensive Health Services, Inc., opened its doors July, 1970 with the hard struggling from Mr. Paul Alston and the Board of Directors. They went about the job of securing grants for operation.

The hiring of the staff was then begun.

Out of this great corporation, three center sites were born. The first was Prospect Hill, next came Chapel Hill – Carrboro, and then the baby of the group, Haywood-Moncure. Haywood-Moncure was opened April 15, 1972. The Center began with four trailers; Mr. Charles Olinger was our first patient. We grew very rapidly, personnel has come and gone and services have increased. We now have thirty-three staff members. Our services now include:

Medical	Dental
Mental Health	X-Ray
Nutrition	Transportation
WIC	Optometry
Pharmacy	Social Services

We would also like to take this opportunity to congratulate nine of our staff members who were there when the doors first opened.

Jean Dowdy	Robena MCrimmon
Rosa Smith	Mary Seymour
Alean Brooks	Rebecca Thompson
Helen Farrar	Sandra Womble
Edna Raines	

This has been a hard struggle, but a pleasant one. The rewards have helped so many families with their needs; socially, physically, mentally, and yes, financially.

We are very proud of the work being done at Haywood-Moncure and by the help of our understanding representatives in our government and above all, God. We will continue this service for mankind.

Daisy Murray

Orange Chatham Comprehensive Health Services

Mr. Paul Alston was working as Executive Director of the Joint Orange Chatham Community Action Agency. He discussed the problems of not having affordable health care in the rural communities of Alamance, Caswell, Lee, Person, Wake, Orange and Chatham counties of North Carolina. Mr. Alston consulted with the University of North Carolina at Chapel Hill, Chapel Hill, North Carolina, and other agencies about this need. Orange Chatham Comprehensive Health Services was incorporated on March 11, 1970. The agency received its first grant on July 1, 1970 to deliver health care services to persons living in the above counties. Out of J.O.C.C.A. birth O.C.C.H.S. which is now named Piedmont Health Care Services, Inc.

I assisted with the funding of O.C.C.H.S. I was first a member of J.O.C.C.A board of directors when Mr. Alston began his visions. Once the vision became a reality, I was chosen to serve in the O.C.C.H.S. board of directors. For the first ten years, I was chairperson of that board. I served on the board for a total of 40 years. In fact, I was the only one that served for that many years. Presently, I am an emeritus board member. My service with the agency was very educational, interesting, business oriented, and joyful. I traveled to many different places and met numerous important people who were a great help to the agency. It was a pleasure to see how many lives we touched through this service.

As submitted by Daisy Murray.

Pictures and Logos

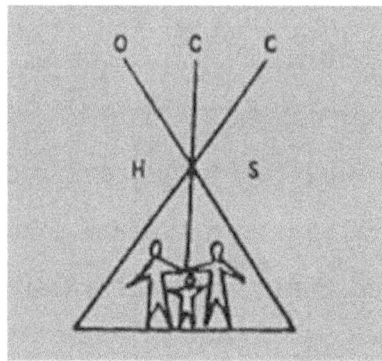

Original Logo for OCCHS

Revised Logo

Early Prospect Hill Community Health Center

First Haywood-Moncure Community Health Center

The Medical Symbol

Jean Dowdy~Marjorie Land~Glenda Hargraves

Carrboro
Community Health Center

Glenda Oldham Hargraves, RN, FNP-C
Time Well Spent

My journey began at Orange Chatham Comprehensive Health Service as an excited nurse of fifteen years, embarking upon a new concept: Nurse Practitioner. This was truly an intoxicating idea. Blazing new trails has always been a part of my "being". Settling in that classroom with those grand ladies of wisdom, I knew my decision was the right one.

There were challenges, but the ones foremost in my mind were the patients' perception of and their acceptance of this new concept and of me. Second, the perception and acceptance of my peers and other medical professionals.

Well, I soon found out, there were those who preferred not to be seen by me because of who I was- a person of color. Even our friends/visitors from other countries were uncomfortable with me as their provider. I vividly recall this family whom I provided care for a family member. After our encounter, the person left the examining room, proceeded to stop a physician in the hall and asked if this was the appropriate treatment. Unaware of my presence, the physician stated "if she examined you and wrote you a prescription for treatment, then it's appropriate." With a smile I retreated to my office.

Another encounter which stands out in my storehouse of memories is, this adorable little boy who told his mother, "I don't want to be touched by a 'nigger' because I don't like them." His mother turned crimson in color and was very apologetic. Maintaining my charm and professionalism we all prevailed. What the young lad didn't know was that I 'had been there' and heard that many times.
The above mentioned are only a few unpleasant incidences. There were many, many more wonderful experiences throughout the 28 years of practice. My heart rejoices when I think of the hundreds of lives I have meaningfully touched.

Often I am stopped with the voices of greetings from those who still remember my 'kindness and understanding. During my tenure at OCCHS/Piedmont Health Services, I had the pleasure of practicing at Prospect Hill Health Center, and at the Haywood Moncure Health Center as well as at the Chapel Hill/Carrboro Health Center. Each center has its uniqueness with gracious, caring, supportive, appreciative and dedicated staff. I can't forget to mention those grand occasions of delicious food and fellowship, which were all absolutely a gustatory delight and soul pleasing.

The drive to Prospect Hill Health Center and to Haywood Moncure Health Center allowed for the contemplative moments with the sights and sounds of the emerging beauty of spring and the peaceful restfulness of the changes of fall. Winter was also lovely, but less calming due to the patches if ice and snow on the roadway.

Of course, all of this could not have happened without the wonderful dedicated people who mentored, nurtured, supported, consoled, comforted and befriended me along the way. Or without the unconditional love of my family who were my ardent supporters. There were also the belief in myself and my spiritual being.

Orange Chatham Comprehensive Health Service, I applaud you and thank you for this opportunity.

As recorded by Glenda Oldham Hargraves, RN, FNP-C

"For I know the plans I have for you,

plans to prosper you and not harm you."

Jeremiah 29:11

Marjorie J. G. Land, RN, FNPC

The first three clinics were located in Chapel Hill-Carrboro, Prospect Hill and Haywood-Moncure, North Carolina.

I first heard about the clinics in the beauty parlor. The founder of the clinics was Mr. Paul O. Alston in cooperation with the UNC School of Medicine, Nursing and Public Health Dentistry. I graduated from North Carolina A&T College – now North Carolina A&T State University, in the 3rd class from the School of Nursing. Mr. Alston's sister was in the class before me. Both classes had members who were hired by NC Memorial Hospital. The hospital actually hired nurses from the first three classes. The Chapel Hill area was not integrated so we lived with families in the black community. Another of his sisters lived there and owned a beauty shop that provided hair care for black women on one side and there was a barber shop on the other side. Several nurses rented rooms in her home and more received hair care in her shop.

It was there that I met Paul O. Alston. He came into the shop and talked with us about his plans to open a Comprehensive Health Center – to staff it with Doctors and Nurse Practitioners. He was the Director of the Orange Chatham Community Action prior to moving to the health program. In his community action work, he noted that people need a basic foundation of health care, housing and education. He was in the process of joining forces with UNC to add the health care piece to the puzzle. He had contributed to the education piece as an educator, housing and education through his community action work. His undergraduate degree from NC A&T College was in Science and Education.

The plan that he and UNC came up with was phenomena. Mr. Alston, UNC School of Nursing, Medicine, Dentistry, and Public Health worked with Orange County, Chatham County, Caswell County and Alamance County; the citizens and politicians to form a coalition to meet their combined needs. He needed health care services for the poor, elderly, and poorly served people. UNC medical, nursing, and dental schools needed patients for their private practices and teaching clinics. The community needed the health care jobs and business.

Mr. Alston talked of their plans to start a Nurse Practitioner Program with UNC School of Nursing, Medicine, Dentistry and Public Health, They wanted experienced nurses so they agreed to pay us the salaries that we were making when we were recruited into the Practitioner Program. We were to go to school for two years in a certificate program to learn to practice medicine under the supervision if physicians. We were trained to practice nursing as registered nurses when we entered the program.

I could not have fantasized a more perfect career ladder for this thirty something years; wife, mother, and nurse who started out too poor to even dream of medical school. Mr. Alston wanted nurses from his alma mater and his community to be in classes from the beginning. I wanted the same. I asked him to include me when he got his program together and he did. But, my husband sons and employer needed a year to adjust to the change. I reluctantly agreed to be in the second class. Sandra Hogan, a Harlem Hospital graduate was in the first class.

When I went into the program, I was making $11,500 a year. Apparently, nurses were not making that kind of money because Public Health Nursing where I had my appointment would not pay me $11,500. But God and the state fixed that! The state gave an across the board raise that brought me up to where I was and God's truth kept marching on.

Our training took place in the School of Nursing classrooms and NC Memorial Hospital Clinics. We were taught by nurses, physicians and health educators and later pharmacists. We had eighteen months of classroom and clinical training.

The last six months was mainly clinical. The health centers were opening in Chapel Hill and Prospect Hill. I was assigned to Chapel Hill-Carrboro, but eventually worked in all three centers.

Mr. Alston had the welfare of his people at heart. His people were the elderly, poor, tired, disenfranchised, underserved, under fed, under housed, and others.

He worked with his contacts in academia mainly but not exclusively, UNC, county government, city government, community action people, regional state and national governments to develop a system of community health/rural health clinics providing comprehensive health care to all people including needy people. This provided jobs for competent health care providers who needed the work. Some needed the work to pay back loans and grants that supported their medical education. This they did through the National Health Services Corporation. Others worked to support themselves. Others had money but wanted to give back to the community – to work with the poor and needy and to experience rural America.

Try to understand that the medical and allied health practitioners listed in the Chapel Hill phone book was perhaps three or four pages or less in the last nineteen sixties – early seventies and this included NC Memorial Professional Staff.

Outside of the hospital was the County Health Department, a few practitioners in Hillsborough. Drs. Jones, Joyner and Patterson's practice, Drs. Senior, Schaffer, and Conley at Chapel Hill Pediatrics, Dr. Rosalind Fergerson on Franklin Street, Dr. Gerbuce Willis somewhere in Chapel Hill, Dr. Thompson on Cameron Avenue, Dr. Hooker and several doctors in Pittsboro-Chatham County, Dr. Siler, Dr. Matheson, Chapel Hill Dermatology, Chapel Hill OB-GYN and Chapel Hill Orthopedics came later.

The "Haves" *(those who have money)* were served in Durham by Lincoln Hospital and private practitioners for Blacks and Watts Hospital for whites and the private practitioners. Duke Hospital served the other black and whites – have and have not.

When Comprehensive Health began to grow – others began to see that it was possible to make a living in the health care industry outside of UNC and perhaps coexist, compliment and support each other.

The OCCHS Boards of Directors had people from county governments, the community and UNC represented. It was an amazing political machine that includes ministers and business people. Mr. Ed Yaggy of NCNB (North Carolina National Bank – now Bank of America) was instrumental in getting our clinic out of UNC Hospital. The clinic moved into NCNB's building on the third floor (I believe). We stayed there until Mr. Yaggy built a building in Carrboro for us and we rented that perhaps long enough to pay for it. The administrative offices were behind the clinic that was in the NCNB building until we moved in the Carrboro building at 105 Roberson Street, Carrboro.

> ***Note:*** *There was a residence at 105 Roberson Street in*
> *Chapel Hill and the mail used to get confused. Mr. and Mrs.*
> *Jacob James lived at 105 Roberson Street in Chapel Hill.*
> *The administrative unit moved to Carrboro with us.*

As his humble undertaking began to become a giant – there developed growingpains. The university and the community began to fight for control it appeared to me. The project was growing not failing. Mr. Alston had to fight to maintain control.

I left OCCHS in 1984 and returned to UNC where I worked the last fifteen years of a forty one year nursing career, twenty-seven as a nurse practitioner totaling forty one years as a registered nurse. I will forever be grateful to the patients' families and health care providers who supported my most fulfilling career.

As submitted by Marjorie Jane Gorham Land
R.N., F.N.P.C.-Retired

Shirley M. Harris

Orange County Comprehensive Health Services, Inc., was organized July 1, 1970 by Paul O. Alston. His goal was to deliver health care services to people living in Orange and Chatham counties and in portions of Alamance, Caswell, Lee, Person, and Wake Counties. The primary emphasis of the program was directed toward the disadvantaged citizens of the area yet to serve the total area residents. Three health centers were built under his directorship; Prospect Hill, Chapel Hill-Carrboro and Haywood Moncure. He provided job opportunities for people living in those health center areas. I, Shirley M. Harris was a recipient of a job opportunity with that agency. On June 13, 1971 I was employed as a Medical Records Clerk for the Haywood Moncure Center. I worked at the main office as a floater waiting for the construction of the Haywood Moncure Center to be completed. However, in the midst of waiting, Marie Drum offered me another position in January 1972 with the agency as Assistant Medical Records Director. Without hesitation and seeing the opportunity to advance, I accepted the position. Shortly after accepting the position, I was enrolled in a Medical Records Technician course. The agency and I contributed half of the tuition. On September 11, 1973, I received my certification as an Accredited Medical Records Technician and later became Director of Medical Records.

The Medical Records Department is a vital area to any medical facility. The purpose of the Medical Records Department is to safeguard patient medical information. The duties included retrieving and filing patient medical records, filing medical information on patients, transcribing medical notes, coding diagnoses, completing insurance forms, release of medical information with authorization and auditing medical records. I supervised and trained people in this area. The job was very challenging because you encountered different situations daily, but I enjoyed it.

I witnessed numerous changes that took place over the year, a new director for the agency, Moses Carey, a name change from OCCHS to Piedmont Health Services Inc., staff changes, new facilities being erected, new policy changes, departments and services added or discontinued, etc. I thank God for the experience of working with Piedmont Health Services for 28 years. It taught me how to facc and overcome any obstacles that may present itself. In January 2000, I resigned from Piedmont Health Services. God has a plan for all of our lives. We never know where it may take us but it will be for the best.

Presently, I am working with UNC Health Care as a Patient Business Associate for the GI Surgery, Chapel Hill, NC. I have been there now for eight years. I enjoy working with my supervisor, physician, nurses, co-workers and especially the patients. I am also able to witness to people about God's goodness and to hear their testimonies, visit and pray with people while they are inpatients at UNC and give encouraging words and inspirational literature. To God be the glory for what He has done in my life.

As submitted by Shirley M. Harris

Dr. Charles Campbell

I met the Director, Mr. Paul Alston, in 1973 while I was attending UNC School of Public Health. Somehow he knew that I was coming to the area before our family arrived. Perhaps, he had learned that I had worked at Matthew Walker Neighborhood Health Center, Nashville, TN.

I began working one day per week for OCCHS at the temporary site on Rosemary Street in the winter of 1974. University of North Carolina Dental School paid my salary. Shortly after I completed the Master in Public Health Program, I was asked by Mr. Alston to organize the Dentist Program at OCCHS. It was necessary that this request be approved by the UNC Dental Ecology Department and the Orange Chatham Comprehensive Health Services Board. There had been two other part-time dental directors: Dr. Drake and Dr. Malone.

Initially, I had to recruit the staff. However, Dr. Sick, a dentist, was already on staff as well as these dental assistants; Sarah Cates, Robena McCrimmon, Carlene and Phyllis Edgerton, and a dental hygienist whose name eludes me now. Mr. Alston and I traveled to several dental schools to recruit dentists: University of North Carolina Dental School, Meharry Medical College School of Dentistry, Howard University and Loma Linda University in California. At first, most of the dentists came from UNC-Chapel Hill and Howard University. We also recruited dental assistants and receptionists.

One aspect of being Dental Director that I appreciated was that I was in a position to help recent graduates get financial start as well as to pay off their school loans. I enjoyed providing care to the patients. I also appreciated the working relationships with the physicians, nurses, pharmacists, dieticians as well as with all of the workers and staff in the program.

I will always treasure the opportunity that I had to work and relate to so many great people.

As recorded by Dr. Charles Campbell
Retired Dental Director OCCHS

Theodore H. Brooks, DDS, MPH

Memories of the Haywood-Moncure Clinic

I, Theodore H. Brooks, DDS, MPH, a recent graduate of Howard University's Dental College, began working for Orange-Chatham Comprehensive Health Services in June,, 1975. After working three months at the dental clinic in Carrboro, I was transferred to the dental clinic at Haywood-Moncure to replace Dr. John Wardsworth, my dental classmate, who was being transferred to the Carrboro dental clinic.

The dental clinic at Haywood-Moncure was operated in a trailer beside the main clinic. Robena McCrimmon was the dental assistant and Sandy Stoker was the hygienist. Another assistant, Hanelore Davis, a Berliner, joined us in 1976. We had no dental receptionist, per se, until 1977 when Celatris Hanner joined us. Upon my arrival, I learned that many patients had been delivered cast partial dentures that were not serviceable. Robena informed such patients to return to the clinic with those dentures and they would be remade at no cost to the patient. That effort continued for over a year until the administration in Carrboro informed us that the procedure could not continue due to limited funds. Also, many patients would appear for emergency treatment five minutes prior to the clinic's closing with the knowledge that they would not be turned away. Robena received overtime pay and as a single person, and new dentist, it mattered little to me (I was only doing what I'd been trained to do). Finally, the administration decided that this could not continue and I realized that if the problem was severe enough, in the patient's mind, they could take off from work to seek treatment.

During my three years at the Haywood-Moncure dental clinic, I had many memorable experiences. There were daily contacts with the likes of Jean Sharpe and Ned Kelly, physicians; Steve Harmon, pharmacist (from whom I learned much); Jean Dowdy, Debra Freeman and Marie Shirley, family nurse practitioners; Rosa Smith and Alean Brooks, clinical assistants; Mary Seymour, receptionist; Stella Headen, intake worker; Rebecca Thompson and Geraldine Hayes, outreach workers; Percy Farrington, driver and many others. During these years, I wrote a column for the Pittsboro Herald on dental matters.

The patients, of all ages, came from the local area generally, but some traveled from as far away as Siler City. Many individuals had never been treated by a dentist before, and as a consequence, I saw many conditions clinically that most dental practitioners only see in text books. E.g., all three entities of Hutchinson's Triad, Scledroderma, Paget's Disease, infections of many recipes, both bacterial and mycosal and several malignant oral lesions and tumors, to mention a few. The majority of these cases were referred to UNC for treatment. It was through a close relationship with Dr. John Jacoway, then Chair of Dept. of Oral Pathology at UNC's Dental School, that these maladies were conclusively from the farm of the patient. Though our patients paid for their services, they still brought us produce, chickens, rabbits, etc. and meals. I assumed this was done out of appreciation for the services we rendered.

In the interest of providing the best care for our patients, Dr. Charles Campbell, then dental director for OCCHS, inaugurated a "peer review" arrangement that, on one day a month, allowed the dentists of OCCHS' three dental clinics (Carrboro, Prospect Hill and Haywood-Moncure) to treat patients in one of the other clinics and evaluate the treatment received by patients there. Dr. Louise Menard was a recent graduate of UNC and worked as a "swing dentist" rendering treatment in all clinics. She frequently worked at Haywood-Moncure.

The three years that I spent at Haywood-Moncure were among the most memorable in my professional career. I believe this was the result of the quality of the persons I had the good fortune to have as coworkers and the uniqueness of the patients that we served. In 1979, when I went back to Carrboro, one of my new co-workers asked if I was glad to be working in Carrboro. I replied that the only thing that I was happy about was that I did not have to commute so far (I lived in Durham), otherwise, I'd rather work at Haywood-Moncure.

As submitted by Theodore H. Brooks, DDS, MPH

Jeffrey Love, D.D.S.

Dental Health Care at Haywood-Moncure Health Center

The position as staff dentist came available in July 1983. At that time, I had just completed a general dentistry residency. This opportunity as dentist allowed me the experience of seeing a large number of patients that would otherwise be seen in an established practice. There was also a variety of needs for the clients seen. Children as well as adults needing prostheses were scheduled. My background in health care had been largely academic, so there were many things I was exposed to at Moncure on a first hand basis.

The first thing I was impressed by was the use of health care as a preventive measure. The experience in Roberson County where I grew up was mainly health care on an emergency basis, except for required examinations. Seeing medical and dental care being received on a preventive basis was different. It also gave new meaning to the training I had received in dental school.

Secondly, I was impressed by the number of minorities that were involved in health care delivery. I sincerely do not remember that community outreach workers and educators being an active part of the health care system in the area around where I grew up. These workers appear to have been very effective based on the number of clients that became enrolled at the clinic.

Finally, my work there helped me to understand that there will probably always be a need for government assistance to the poor and untrained. The cost of services would not have been affordable to most of the clients without some type of assistance or decreased fees. The challenge that goes hand in hand with this is who ultimately pays for the difference in fees. There will also be the equal challenge of what cost is there when the places like Moncure cease to exist. The center certainly made a difference in the many surrounding counties. I wished there could have been one in my home town when I was growing up.

As submitted by Dr. Jeffrey Love

Robena McCrimmon

Around the end of December 1971, I was working at the Koury Company. I received a call and was asked to come in for an interview for a dental assistant position. The interviewer said "we are not supposed to hire relatives in this program, so if you do not tell anyone that you and Rosa are sisters, I will not. Now if you work anything like Rosa, I am hiring a hard working person."

I began working with Orange Chatham Comprehensive Health Service (OCCHS) in January 1992. I was trained on the job as well as taking a dental assistant course at the University of North Carolina Dental School, Chapel Hill, NC. Then OCCHS built a dental facility in Carrboro, NC that served the medical and dental needs of the patients. They later built a dental facility in Prospect Hill, NC. All dental assistants that worked for OCCHS had to travel to each location to work for a period of time. No one picked Monday so that was my day. Monday, oh how I hated blue Monday (smile)!

Years later OCCHS opened a dental facility in Moncure, NC. That was my clinic. My traveling days were over. The dental clinic helped a lot of people, including my family and I. There were many times people would come in so afraid and we would remove a tooth and they would not know the tooth had been extracted. They would come in crying and leave out smiling. I learned a lot and gained an excellent work experience. By the time the Moncure clinic was opened, everyone knew that Rosa and I were sisters. Some secrets just cannot be kept.

As submitted by, Robena McCrimmon

Dr. Steve N. Almond

I was serving on the faculty at the School of Pharmacy, UNC when I was offered an opportunity in 1972 to establish a pharmacy in a rural health center being set up to serve Chatham County citizens. I felt that a joint appointment in which I would continue my work at the University and also practice pharmacy at Haywood-Moncure Community Health Center would be nearly ideal. I would have the pleasure of providing pharmacy services to patients and other members if a health care team and at the same time, the experiences of doing what would enhance my teaching of pharmacy students.

"Health care team" is a key term. The OCCHS endeavor together with a group of people from a wide range of backgrounds and with an equally wide range of knowledge and talents. It didn't take long working together on a common mission to learn that each of the individuals who would form our team possessed to their colleagues and to the patients we would serve. Those colleagues turned out to be some of the finest people with whom I have worked, and I continue to hold them dearly today.

Some Memories

When I first arrived at what was to become the Haywood-Moncure Community Health Center, I was surprised to see that the clinic "building" was three of four trailers joined together. I was even more surprised when I was shown the room that had been assigned to be the pharmacy. If I remember correctly, its size was almost five feet by ten feet. It didn't take a math major to calculate that, once one-foot deep drug storage shelves lined each of the three walls, the remaining work space would be only three feet by nine feet....hardly enough space to even turn around, much less work efficiently. Negotiations with administrators resulted in the pharmacy being set up in a room twice as wide.

Miss Edna Earl Raines was the appointment clerk and her desk was just outside the pharmacy. At times when her workload was not too heavy, she would volunteer to help me in the pharmacy. We worked well together and she provided me with much needed technical assistance. After a time, Edna elected to move from her original position to become a pharmacy technician. She went to UNC for technician training and gained a certificate acknowledging her completion of the course. We worked together in the pharmacy for almost twelve years.

I had worked closely with the physicians at the hospital at UNC, and was accustomed to pooling our respective areas of expertise to ensure the best possible outcomes for patients in our care. Although I had participated in teaching those in the nurse practitioner classes at UNC about drug products and drug therapies, I had never worked in practice with a nurse practitioner. As such, I had little idea what to expect from that newly developed category of health professionals. Two of the original FNP's at Haywood-Moncure were Jean Dowdy and Ruth Efird. I remember first meeting Jean and speaking with her, but I don't remember what she said. I don't remember because, upon meeting her, I was somewhat stunned. Captivated by her radiant smile, I decided (probably less than a second) that standing before me was one of the most beautiful women I had ever seen. I soon learned as I worked with jean that her friendliness and professional standards were right in line with her beauty. They too, were top notch. I remember well going with Jean to the home of a diabetic patient whose reported symptoms were consistent with hypoglycemia. We arrived and found her unresponsive. After a quick assessment, jean administered glucose IV and the patient regained consciousness within a minute or less. It's likely that her life was saved by that visit.

Ruth's last name had caught my attention. The only Efirds I had known were from my native county (Stanly), and I wondered about her origin. It turned out that she was married to Rick Efird, a Stanly county native who was a pharmacist and was a faculty member at the School of Pharmacy in my Division. It was only after meeting Ruth that I learned of the connection. Her personality was such that working with her was like working with an old friend, even though I had known her for just a short time at the beginning, My experience with the nurse practitioners was rewarding both professionally and personally. From our working together, our patients received a level of care that would not have been available to them otherwise.

Then there was the time Ned, a dedicated physician somewhat behind in seeing patients on that busy day, stopped for a quick bite to eat at lunch time. He hurriedly grabbed what he thought was his lunch from the refrigerator and gulped it down, only to learn upon tasting it after a few swallows that it was lunch, but someone else's and it had been in the refrigerator for a l-o-n-g time. Ned had a dilemma. He had to see his increasing number of patients, but he dared not suffer the effects of food that he suspected might have contained botulism or other natural toxins. What could he do? He took a dose of ipecac syrup and carrying an emesis basin, went on to see the next patient. I believe he finished that patient and stepped out back before receiving the benefit of his ipecac therapy.

Dave McKay, M.D. and his 1961 Mercedes Benz 190SL roadster; I coveted that car. It made my 1964 MG roadster look like...well...an MG. After driving it to the clinic for a few years, one day Dave showed up in another car. I asked about the Mercedes and he said he had it repainted and sold it to a woman for $6,000 and he appeared to feel somewhat guilty for having charged her so much. My mouth must have dropped open. In any case, my heart dropped a bit. I had not even known it was for sale. Probably just as well, as I doubt I could have gotten a loan for that amount on a car that was more than twelve years old. I would have tried though. A check of the literature revealed that '61 190SL's were selling for $10,000 to $15,000 at that time. Dr. Sam Putnam, MD, I found to be a truly unique individual. He showed himself to be a knowledgeable physician, a brilliant teacher, and a man who did not mind getting his hands dirty cleaning the clinic and the parking lot. Sam always served others before himself. He enjoyed simple pleasures. Though a New Yorker, Sam was in his element at the Moncure clinic.

And there was Dr. Sam Tipton, MD, a Tennessee mountain man and physician with whom it was a great pleasure to work with. Despite the fact that he came from the School of Medicine at Duke, he jumped in and worked with all of the UNC people whose numbers predominated at the clinic.

Sandra, Wanda, Mary, Helen, Maida, Vallie, Lucille, Alean (both, even though they're spelled differently), Barbara, Deborah, Paul, Greg, Jean C., Mimi, Percy, Charles and the many others. We felt like family and friends and worked together that way. Sometimes there were ups and downs, but usually there was harmony. Patient care was our primary concern, but we had fun too.

Among the pleasant memories is one that is less that pleasant, but in its own way, is rather humorous. The entire original cast, no doubt, remembers that the bathroom was in the middle of the trailer of the clinic and that put it in the of the clinic adjacent to the lab, the hallway and the pharmacy. The overhead fluorescent lights in the trailers were three feet long, and there were openings in the hall at the ceiling level through which the lights passed from room to room, including the bathrooms. Well, light was not the only thing that made that passage. Occasionally there were vapors emanating from the central bathroom that made the surrounding small rooms seem even smaller that they were, particularly when the patient had a gastrointestinal disorder. The bathroom music was an additive as well. Sometimes the combination made serious patient counseling and patient education about their drug therapies a real challenge.

As submitted by Steve N. Almond

Jean Chapman, M.D.

When I moved to North Carolina from my pediatric residency in NYC's South Bronx, I carried the name of Dr. Evi Schmidt and the word that she directed a health center for people "pushed to the edge" in the area I was about to call home. "We aren't looking for a pediatrician right now" she said, "but why don't you go talk to Mr. Paul Alston?" I did, and the rest is history.

Mr. Alston and I sized each other up and said, "This works!" OCCHS was just about to hire their first non-UNC-contract physician---and I was it. Paul's passion for a commitment to underserved communities in Chatham County was just what I'd been hoping to find. The rural South was home to me and generations of my living-on-the-edge farm ancestors for time out of mind, and it felt like coming home. I began work in April of 1975, and OCCHS <u>was</u> home to me for eleven years.

There are no words for what I learned in those years: our families taught me about strength, and how it is to be marginalized and how that plays itself out in health, growth and development-they taught me humility, and how to parent and how to love and how to make it, and –oh yes- how to do pediatrics. And my beloved co-workers taught me all of that and more about community and hanging on, about faith, and being in the struggle for the long haul, about integrity, about racism and classicism and poverty, about joy and grief and loyalty. If I started naming all those who were teachers, I'd never end and I'd forget someone so I won't even begin. We were in the trailers, then Mr. Percy Farrington drove out every morning and brought folks in.

Medical Records was the hub and heart where we all hung out. How Steve Almond (Pharmacist) sat on that tiny stool, made a desk of a briefcase on his knee, and taught me so much about medicines and good care—I'll never truly understand. Mrs. Madie Lynch and Mrs. Vallie Alston, Mrs. Lucille Holder, Mrs.

Rebecca Thompson and Mrs. Miriam Stone were our day to day outreach in the communities, but then, so were nearly all the staff. We were sort of out in the middle of nowhere – some brave souls sometimes trekked to Deep River Restaurant for lunch but mostly we happily squeezed shoulder-to-shoulder in the little break room over our lunches from home. (Mary Seymour could always go home for lunch since she lived next door.) Some folk then, and now, would say – "Oh, we've got all white doctors and nurse practitioners and dentists because you just can't find people of color for those positions. Well, I always use Mr. Paul Alston as an example, for Paul that was a priority so he <u>looked</u> and he <u>found</u> people of color for those positions, and that was a big part of our strength, of being what's now called an "anti-racist organization", Paul just did it – and everyone helped, well maybe almost everyone.

Sure there were problems and conflicts but you know those pale over the years and what remains, is knowing your part of building something good and caring, professional and compassionate for and with the community, my first and best teachers. Thanks OCCHS!

As submitted by Jean Chapman, M.D.

Samuel R. Tipton, Jr. M.D.

Since I left the Moncure Clinic in 1984, I got a job in Saudi Arabia working as a GP at a clinic for the big oil company there until 1995. Then I moved back to Knoxville, TN, which is where I grew up and went to grammar and high school. In 1995, I got a job there at the University of Tennessee Student Health Center taking care of the students until I retired from work in 2001. Now I still live in Knoxville, but I do a lot of international travel, mostly bird watching. I've traveled to Australia, Central and South America, Europe and next year I hope to go to Africa. I have stayed in touch with Marie and Jack Shirey who live in Boone, North Carolina and from time to time, Greg Lee and I correspond; he lives in the Raleigh area. I rarely get the Chapel Hill area anymore.

Let me give some of my thoughts about the Moncure Clinic as I have very fond memories of my three years there. Growing up in the south in the strict segregation days of the 1940-1970 periods gave me a strong feeling as a young white boy that something was not right, and an uneasy feeling about racial relations in the south began to grow in me. As the Civil Rights Movement grew and Martin Luther King, Jr. began to lead the south in new direction, I became more hopeful that changes could occur. In 1968 as I was about to graduate from medical school in Memphis, Tennessee, Martin Luther King, Jr. was suddenly killed. It upset me so much I swore that I would leave the south for better places. I moved to Washington, DC for two years and then to the San Francisco Bay area for eight years. In 1979, I missed the south a lot and decided to move back and ended up in Chapel Hill, North Carolina where I happened to meet Paul Alston one day. He and I had a common interest in community and neighborhood health centers and he invited me to start working at the Orange Chatham Community Health Service (OCCHS). I worked at the Carrboro Clinic and the Prospect Hill Clinic until 1981 when I started working full time at the Moncure Health Center.

For the first time in my career, I felt like I had finally found my place. Here was rural medicine in a racially mixed region of the south where people worked closely together in a small clinic with a lot of respect and caring for each other, the way medical care should be in this country. The staff and patients were racially mixed and those issues didn't seem to matter anymore. We had good physicians and great nurse practitioners who worked closely together to give high quality and caring primary care the way it should be done. With a supporting staff of folks from the nearby communities and a great pharmacy and dental clinic, the Moncure Health Center provided the best health care to the region that I have been a part of before or since. It was truly a healing place for me as well as our patients and also a fun place to work. Unfortunately, in the 1980's the funding began to fade and the staff began to leave. I left in 1984, but I have always felt since then that it was the best place that I worked throughout my career, and I often wished that I could recreate it. Those three years were the peak of my medical career!

As submitted by Samuel R. Tipton, Jr. M.D.

Marie Shirey, FNP

In 1974, my husband and I and our son moved to Moncure, North Carolina. Our younger son, Will had a fever and I took him to the clinic. Fortunately, he was seen by Jean Dowdy, the first FNP I had ever met, I was very impressed with her professionalism and her friendly style. She was more than happy to explain her FNP education and soon I had an appointment with the clinic's director, Mr. Paul Alston. By 1975-1976, I was in the UNC-Chapel Hill FNP program. My internship at Moncure was wonderful and everyone on the staff was most helpful. Jean Dowdy taught me a lot of things I had learned in school. She and others helped me refine my skills. I have always felt that my years in Moncure were the key to my love for my twenty-six year career as an FNP. I owe so much to all of the Moncure staff and I will always count them as dear friends.

Wanda	Administrator
Sandra	Front Desk and Administrator
Mary	Front Desk
Helen	Medical Records
Geraldine	Medical Records
Melanie	Medical Transcriptions
Rosa, Alene and Mildred	Clinical Assistants
Jean Dowdy, Jessie Goins	FNP's
Deborah Freeman and Gay Kayye	FNP's
Ned Kelly, Jean Sharpe, Dave McKay	MD's
Sam Tipton, Barbara Williams	MD's
Peter Pompei and Dr. Gallagher	MD's
Dr. Wilson	Psychiatrist
Fred Summers	OB-GYN
Steve Almond	Pharmacist
Edna Raines	Pharmacy Assistant
Mr. Percy Farrington	Driver and handyman

The "home visit" time built into the weekly schedule provided many unforgettable experiences. My patients and their families taught me many things about life, people and living day to day.

So, Haywood-Moncure, thanks for the memories.

As submitted by Mary Shirey, FNP

Deborah Underwood Brown (Freeman) FNP, RN
Remembering the Haywood-Moncure Community Health Center -- 1976-1989

As I walked into the back door my first day at the Haywood-Moncure Community Health Center in 1976, I could see only the modular units connected by wooden ramps that made a hollow sound as I walked between the rooms, the sparely furnished rooms, the minimum of medical equipment and my own inexperience as a new graduate of the Nurse Practitioner program at UNC Chapel Hill.

Little did I know that day, of the rich learning environment, as I would be mentored by the many skilled physicians, and nurse practitioners. I did not know then of the patients who would teach me, and give me far more than I could ever teach or give to them. I was naively unaware of the wisdom of the community health workers who would over the next 14 years teach me the importance of respect, and seeing the whole person not just the disease.

The faces of patients, flood my mind as I recall my work at Moncure. I can remember the names one by one:

The woman who was blind, had renal impairment and had a double amputation due to diabetes. We care for her at home for everything from necrosis to pneumonia. The man who was brought in with both feet necrotic and sticking to his boots from freezing while in a ditch unconscious from alcohol. The heart attacks, the snakebites, the children with high fevers and the frightened parents, and the 8 year old boy who was a frequent walk-in, with everything from a pebble in his ear, to a splinter 8 inches long in his buttock from sliding down a makeshift slide made of plywood. Oh yes, and the elderly woman who was brought to us weekly by her very large boys for penicillin injections for tertiary syphilis. She would not get out of the car, so we gave her the shots in the car with the boys holding her down. What a sight! I cannot leave out the woman with a wolf spider in her ear; who ran out of the clinic screaming "Lordy Jesus" after the spider crawled over her face and escaped to the floor as I poured water in her ear.

The stories of tigers and penicillin in Malaysian, delivering babies at "The Farm" from doctors with experience that could not be taught from a book or learned in a hospital. Clinical "pearls" passed on then, still with me as I examine patients today.

I recall the atmosphere of "family" within our clinic. The wonderful meals of tender turnip greens, creasy greens (I still do not know how to spell that word), chicken and oh my, the desserts that would melt in your mouth. I will never forget the love and support within those staff meetings. The way everyone rallied to help when anyone was going through a bad time.

The community was a network that looked out for each other, and depended on us for medical support as well as social support. I never felt afraid as I traveled the deep back woods of Chatham and Lee counties, walking often the last dirt path to the house of an elderly patient with pneumonia, or checking on a newborn in a house with cracks in the clapboards so wide that snow was piled on the floor inside the house.

Many years have passed since those rich, wonderful times in Moncure, but I can still feel the warmth, and see the faces of those wonderful people in the clinic and the patients. I am thankful to have been a little part of it all.

As submitted by Deborah Underwood Brown (Freeman)

Loretta Dowdy ~ Marjorie Land ~ Glenda Land

Jessie Kelly-Holmes, RN, FNP

Opening a New Door

Driving into the parking lot at Orange-Chatham Comprehensive Health Services in 1978, I noticed all the cars already in the parking lot at 7:30 a.m. The clinic was in a rural area of Chatham County, just down the road from Moncure, NC, and there were more cars in the parking lot that would equal the few small homes I had passed on the way there. I found out later that not only did the clinic serve the people from Chatham County but many people came from surrounding counties because of the clinic's reputation for delivering excellent health care, its' sliding scale fee for services and its' affiliation with UNC Hospital at Chapel Hill, I could only imagine how busy my first day would be.

I was starting my preceptorship for 6 months, before I could finish the Family Nurse Practitioner Program at the School of Nursing at UNC., the rotation was necessary. This would also be the area of employment for me after graduation. I met Marie Shirley in the parking lot and we went in together.

Already there were people checking in at the front desk. There were three people behind the desk gathering information on each individual. I was introduced to each one and greeted cordially, and followed Marie into Medical Records and introductions were made. When I saw the number of records on the shelves , I was astonished. Then I was told that these records were not only for medical but for the dental clinic as well. I was in awe that the Haywood-Moncure clinic included a Pharmacy with a Pharmacist and Technician, a lab, an x-ray department with the medical clinic with three full-time Family Nurse Practitioners (I was the fourth), two full-time Adult Care Physicians, a Pediatrician, two Health Educators, and all the support staff and its' services including transportation for patients within a certain radius, to and from the clinic.

I had met Paul Alston, the Project Director, only once prior to this and had no idea his vision was so great. Now viewing all that was available in the rural health clinic, I realize what an awesome challenge he must have had because there were a total of three clinics under the Orange-Chatham Comprehensive Health Services umbrella and all with the same services available.

The staff was wonderful helpful, and inspiring. I had never worked with such a large group of people that were focused on the same goal, "helping and serving the patients of Orange-Chatham Comprehensive Health Clinic" no matter their residential location, ethnic background, or financial status. The staff was professional, always ready to give insight and never afraid to go the step beyond what the more to give the patient the best care.

In the years that followed, I enjoyed the expertise of all the staff that was so willing to share, so willing to teach, and so eager to encourage and support each other. The patients were not seen as "my" patient or "your" patient, but were viewed as "our" patients and were given the benefits of all the professionals involved in their care. Each day was a new adventure. Each provider had a daily schedule but unexpected situations were a given for any day. I found comfort in knowing that whatever walked through the doors of the clinic, the group of people with whom I worked, would assist me in handling it.

One day I arrived at the clinic early, which was usual for me because I enjoyed my job so much, and I found a young female and her husband in the parking lot in their vehicle. She was on the backseat in active labor he came running across the parking lot to me before I could get my car stopped, "my wife is having a baby," he said. I got out of my vehicle and went over to the car. She was in the backseat with her legs up in position and pushing. A few moments later, thank God, the person providing transportation pulled up and opened the clinic door so I could use the phone to call EMS (this was before cell phones), EMS arrived shortly and off she went to the hospital at Chapel Hill in their capable hands. Boy what a way to start the day! I refrained from getting to work earlier than the rest of the staff after that.

There were so many interesting and challenging events that occurred while working at Orange-Chatham Comprehensive Health Services, from counseling a mother with a pregnancy with an Ana cephalic fetus that was doomed to die, to managing the care of a patient with a Priprisam that was afraid because he did not know what to expect. These extraordinary experiences, with knowledgeable professionals always available, gave me a powerful self-confidence that I have used continuously since.

I have frequently recalled my experiences with the staff and patients to many groups over the years. The stories are too numerous to continue in this brief summary. I do recall one incident in particular after I left Haywood-Moncure, when I was unable to resuscitate a young man after he had been electrocuted by a laser. He was treated at a local hospital and returned to work. I was rewarded with a visit from the upper management, and I told one of them I did not see the point in extra recognition for this since "I felt I was just doing my job", and he said, "A lot of people know how to help, but how many can or will if it is necessary?"

I will forever treasure the compelling, impressive, and passionate era in my professional and personal life at the Orange-Chatham Comprehensive Health Services and at the Haywood-Moncure Clinic. I will forever remember the staff and the patients. Whatever name is used to describe the clinic, whatever walks through the doors, the quality of care will always be EXCELLENT!

As submitted by Jessie Kelly-Holmes, RN, FNP
1977-1983 Haywood-Moncure Health Clinic

Jean Dowdy, RN, FNP, BA

It was a feeling of indescribable success, joy, and pride, as Paul Alston, contemplated on the trials and challenges he had incurred prior to the opening of the Prospect Hill Health Center. This center was located in Prospect Hill, North Carolina. You see, this giant of a man was very knowledgeable with a soft heart. He was a classmate of an uncle of mine at the A&T University. My uncle said that he was a quiet man. One day in class my uncle stated that the instructor asked Mr. Alston a question concerning the lesson. Not only did Mr. Alston answer the question but he also went into great detail to explain the answer.

Mr. Alston's degrees were in Education and Health Services and he had worked in the school system for many years. In this calling, he saw many poor children with rashes, colds, and pneumonia, whose parents had no transportation or money to pay for the doctor visits or prescriptions. After retiring from the school system, he got busy and with the help of many individuals and the University of North Carolina at Chapel Hill, he was able to get a grant for millions of dollars from the Office of Economic Opportunity. The Board of Directors was established. Mr. Kemp Jones was President of the board. Other members were Dr. Arden Mille, father of Dr. Thomas (Tom), Mr. Artemous Wilson, father of Mr. Cecil Wilson, and Mrs. Daisy Murray, now Ex-officio, a very dedicated individual. The organization was named the Orange-Chatham Comprehensive Health Services. At the board meetings Edwin Caldwell represented Orange-Chatham Comprehensive Health Services and Moses Carey represented the School of Public Health and the University. The professors from the School of Public Health, the medical school, the School of Pharmacy and the Associate professors from the School of Nursing and support staff from different communities, community health workers, drivers for transportation were enough to open three health centers. Community Health Workers were assigned to

FNP's. The FNP's and Community Health workers assigned to see patients within a ten mile radius of the health center. Transportation picked up patients from different areas in the community to bring them to the health center. The patients were also transported to NC Memorial Hospital for routine appointments. Lab work was sent to the Central Office in Carrboro. Patient scheduling was matched with the transportation pick up. Our Community Health Workers worked very hard in the community to define who we were and what we were all about. Lucille Holden told me that one of the potential patients in her area said to her that they thought the health center was for colored people only, but she soon cleared that up. Drs. Axalla Hoole, Robert Greenberg, and Glenn Pickard, Jr. wrote the patients care guidelines for Nurse Practitioners.

Prospect Hill Community Health Center, Prospect Hill, NC

Lead Physician – Glenn Pickard

Unit Manager – Ann Sawyer

FNP's – Betty Compton, Margaret Wilkman

Carrboro Community Health Center, Carrboro, NC

Lead Physician – Axalla Hoole

Unit Manager – Dororthea Farrington

FNP's – Glenda Hargraves, Marjorie Land, Sandra Hogan

Haywood-Moncure Community Health Center, Moncure, NC

Lead Physician – Samuel Putnam

Unit Manager – John Holland

FNP's – Hattie Nagel, Ruth Efird, Elene Fuller, Jean Dowdy

Community Health Workers – Rebecca Thompson, Madie Lynch, Lucille Holden   Rosa Smith, Vallie Alston, Mirian Stone, Geneva Parker

Driver – Oscar Cotton

Pharmacist – Steve Almond

Pharmacy Technician – Edna Raines

Intake Worker/Appointments – Mary Seymour, Sandra Womble

Clinical Assistant – Alean Brooks

Lab Technician – Barbara Eaves

The Carrboro Community Health Center opened with few problems.

When Haywood-Moncure opened, it was fairly normal because we had many dry runs. The center opened into a small trailer. I was excited and frightened to death. However, when I met my first patient, a handsome baby boy named Brian Cross, the son of the Rev. Cathy Jones, I was relieved.

One of the most embarrassing things that happened to me was one day a mother brought her son into the center for a physical and I as I started to sit down, the chair slipped and I sat on the floor. I thought that family would never stop laughing. I tried to compose myself and look professional, but that was very hard to do.

The most exciting thing that happened in this practice was when a teenaged pre-natal near term called in to say she was having pressure. She was advised to come in for a check. She was checked in as I was finishing up with another patient. I gave her a gown. I measured the fetus, listened to its heartbeat and assisted her into the stirrups. After I had gloved to check her cervix, I found there was no cervix because the infant was crowning. Dr. Thomas Miller was in the lunchroom having his lunch. One of the Clinical Assistants got him in a hurry and he delivered the beautiful little infant –wow!

One of the most frightening and sad occasions was the weekend, on Saturday, when some of the communist workers party was killed in Greensboro, NC. One of our physicians was there and her fiancé' was killed. The Haywood-Moncure Community was in an uproar. Patients refused to come back to the clinic. The KKK graffiti was across the front of the building. One of the store owners said to me, "I didn't know you all were communist up there." It took a long time for things to get back to a sense of normalcy. The corporation and the University split. Haywood-Moncure had no physicians.

Physicians were flown from Washington, DC daily to give care. One of the doctors said to me that he did not trust the care given by FNPs. I said to him, "I disagree with you doctor, because I have patient care guidelines I have to follow and I know what I'm doing and I know where my limitations lie. If I need you, I will cal you." He was not certified to supervise FNPs, so if I needed a physician, I would call Dr. Pickard. FNPs took calls at night for a week at a time with back-up physicians taking second calls. We would go on home visits into our assigned areas with community health workers and our equipment bag which was orange.

On a Tuesday in September, the day after Labor Day weekend, 1981, a deputy sheriff from Chatham police department appeared at my office door. He presented a summons for me to appear at Chatham County court concerning a wrongful birth case. There was a lady that had given birth to a baby boy that had Down's syndrome. Not only was I involved, but also Orange Chatham Comprehensive Health Services, and the backup OB-GYN Physician from the University of North Carolina at Chapel Hill, North Carolina. At that point-in-time, amniocentesis was done at age thirty-seven; unless there was a history, a high level of concern or other genetic disorders. The lady in question was a thirty-five or thirty-six year old. When she asked me about amniocentesis, I referred her to the OB back up physician.

The Trial

After eight days of testimony it was revealed that the patient stated that the physician told her the upswing for Down's Syndrome was around thirty-seven years of age. She also stated; that nothing that Jean Dowdy had said to her would have prevented her from seeking treatment.

There was a policy change for the whole community. Every hospital in the area started to refer OB patients at fifteen weeks gestation if thirty-five years of age to genetic counseling or before if necessary. Later there was a blood test developed that screens for Down's Syndrome at fifteen weeks gestation. The name of the test is called Alpha Fetal protein Screening. If positive, the patient is referred to genetic counseling and/or amniocentesis. This was a very complicated situation that turned out to be very positive and powerful outcome for all OB patients.

As submitted by Jean Dowdy, RN, FNP, BA

I Won't Complain

I had some good days

I had some hills to climb

I had some weary days and

Some sleepless nights,

But when I look around

And think things over

All of my good days

Outweigh my bad days

I won't complain.

Sometimes the clouds hang low

I can hardly see the road,

I ask the question Lord

Why so much pain,

But he knows what's best for me

Although my weary eyes, they can't see

I'll just say thank you Lord

I won't complain.

Lyrics by Rev. Paul Jones

Sandra Hogan, RN, FNP

Sandra Hogan was the first class of Family Nurse Practitioners from the UNC School of Nursing at Chapel Hill, North Carolina. Sandra was interviewed for this position by Martha Gorst. She was assigned to work at Carrboro Health Center. Margaret Wilkerson and Betty Compton, also in the first class, were assigned to Prospect Hill Health Center.

The first standing orders were written by the first class if Nurse Practitioners in consultation with Dr. Pickard, Dr. Axalla Hoole, Dr. Robert Lawrence, and Dr. Greenburg.

The Carrboro Health Center started in Modular D at North Carolina Memorial Hospital, Chapel Hill, North Carolina. Sandra and Dorothea Farrington (unit manager), hired the clinical staff and community health workers.

Sandra writes that she went many places with Dr. Sam Putnam to publicize the concept of Family Nurse Practitioners because the North Carolina Nurses Association was afraid FNPs were going to be "mini doctors". Other places of visitation were the Veteran's Hospital and the local newspaper.

Another interview was done with Dr. Frank Loda, the Dean of the UNC School of Nursing; Lucy Conant, Paul Alston, and others. Dr. Loda gave Sandra "a bit of a hard time". When she got home, she started to question herself about what had she gotten herself into. She called a person that was at the meeting and was reassured.

All and all, our instructors and supervisors treated us with respect.

As submitted by Sandra Hogan, RN, FNP- Carrboro Health Center

Ruth Kaemmerlen Efird – Nurse Practitioner

My Life Education at Moncure Health Center

I was very fortunate to be trained as a nurse practitioner in 1970 at UNC through funds from rural health designated for Moncure Health center. After a 4 month academic program at UNC through the medical nursing schools I started practicing at the new Prospect Hill, and then the new Chapel Hill health Center, while the health facility at Moncure was being constructed. Several months before Moncure opened the new health team began to interview people through JOCCA (the community action organization) for openings as community health workers, pharmacy aides, lab aides, and secretaries. None of these people had any medical training, but knew the community well, especially the health needs. It was fun to train some of them in how to take vital signs, draw blood, and test urine specimens, prepare and clean exam rooms, and prepare meds. They taught us how to respect all types of people, how to visit them in their home environments, use rat traps and insect pesticide strips, and use medicines without proper refrigeration. These people would accompany us on home visits, publicize the clinical services, deliver medicines, and give us suggestions on how best to get cooperation for treatment needs.

My love for public health for all people came from the wonderful people I encountered in both Chatham and Lee Counties. Even though I had medical education, my patients taught me how to modify health plans to fit each particular situation: illiteracy, poor sanitation, lack of refrigeration, rodent infestation, lack of money and transportation, and chronic disease conditions that were not first priority in many instances. In other words, I got an education in the real world that many people face every day. Some of my patients worked for a local chicken plant, and couldn't come for appointments for their diabetes and high blood pressure evaluations. They would run out of medicines because if they left work for the health center the whole factory process would have to be shut down and many people would lose their pay. So we learned to take the medicines to the people, draw their blood during breaks at the job, to keep them working and healthy. I even remember making home visits to clean wounds, draw blood, take out medicines, and do exams on those too disabled to come in to the center. Other could not read so we would draw pictures as to when to take medicines. The goals was to keep as many as possible out the hospitals, and to educate them to take medicines provided at the center, as well as eat better, within budgetary limitations.

During this time money was available to improve living conditions in homes of the people who came to the center. New trailers were built. Indoor bathrooms were installed. We were involved in training what should and should not be flushed down the toilets to avoid plumbing problems and to improve sanitation with hand washing.

The nurse practitioner and doctors took turns being on call 24 hours a day, seven days a week. There were very few calls because people were not used to having someone available, not seeing the necessity for care unless there was an emergency. We did learn how to suture and occasionally that became very helpful to people who had only been used to washing the wound and wrapping it.

I have become very active in the right to health care for all people as a result of this wonderful experience. I later worked at Orange County Health Department for 30 years as a nurse practitioner to continue providing health care to those without private health insurance. I am grateful to the people in Chatham and Lee Counties, as well as the people who worked at Moncure, for the real world health teaching they gave to me. Recently, in 2010 President Obama and the US Congress passed a health care bill to provide health insurance for all citizens. I am so proud that I have lived to see this important step in equality of health care to all!

As submitted by Ruth Kaemmerlen Efird

Rosa Smith – Community Health Worker

I was working with the Moncure Community Program when Mr. Paul Alston called me into his office and talked to me about starting a Piedmont Health Program and one question he asked was; "Do you think it would work?" My answer was yes. So I started contacting the people in the community. Some people wanted it and some did not. After the program got started and people found out all that was offered in the program it was a different story. They were glad to have a Community Health Center in the city of Moncure and so was I. Today we have a medical center and doctors and nurses and we all are proud of the Moncure Health Center.

I also took patients to shop for groceries because they had no transportation, to Social Security and meetings held nightly. I worked in the clinic as a clinical assistant checking height, weight, temperature, drawing blood, and finger sticks.

As submitted by Rosa Smith

Martha L. Holden, Community Health Worker

On April 13, 1972, I was going back to school at Central Carolina Technical Institute in Sanford, NC; taking some classes related with nursing and medical assistant. I was taking these classes at night and while working in the Intensive Care Unit (ICU) at the hospital on Saturdays. Unfortunately, I didn't have driver's licenses and had never driven an automobile until I was almost finished with my classes. Towards the end of my studies I enrolled in drivers training, passed the road and written exam and was awarded my license.

One day while I was just sitting around doing nothing special, Dr. Samuel Putnam and Ruth Efird stopped by to see me. We chatted for a period of time and they told me about future plans to open a health center in Moncure, NC. This center would be about five miles from my home. Dr. Putnam asked me if I would be interested in going back to school, getting more training so that I could work at the clinic. I told him that since my husband was paralyzed and in a wheelchair, I wasn't sure, but I would discuss it with my husband and get back with him at a later time. My husband thought this was a good chance for me to have a career in the field I loved, taking care of the sick. Therefore, I was very excited to tell Dr. Putnam yes!

A study group was started on January 31, 1972; we studied a variety of things about nursing and social work. We ended this phase of special training in April of 1972 and opened the doors of the new clinic on April 13, 1972. The first day Dr. Putnam called it a "dry run" practice. We started off with community health workers, which we called CHW. Our role was to meet with the Family Nurse Practitioners. Including me there were six community health workers: Vallie Alston, Elizabeth Alston, Madie Lynch, Rosa Smith, Mirian Stone, and Rebecca Thompson. Our first job was to be assigned to certain areas in and around the county and go out and recruit people, telling them about the clinic and what the clinic had to offer them in the way of patient care.

We told them that we were no trying to take them from their doctors if they had one, but to offer our services if they did not have a doctor. We explained that they could get very good care at our clinic at reduced prices. We told them to bring in some form of identification and proof of income. At this time; they would register to become our patients. Their fee would be based upon the number in the family and their income. I had Loretta Jean Dowdy, FNP as my supervisor. We did not know what we might run across when we went out into the field, but we met a lot of friends and many became patients. After this, the client would come in and be seen by our doctors and then their FNP. Each patient had an FNP for their area.

Routinely, we health workers would go out to their home and take their blood pressure, check urine, sugar, and read tuberculosis tests. We each had a ten mile radius that we covered. We also could collect urine for pregnancy tests. The patient would then call or come by for the results. I had two rest homes in my area and as far as I know some are still patients at the clinic. Some of the patients were across the county line in Wake County. As CHWs, we were supposed to try to visit as many as four patients per day. We would then come back to the clinic and make a requisition for each patient's chart. All of the information gathered would be confidential. Many times I would be called at night to answer a question from a patient or go out and check on them. I did not mind this because I loved my job and the patients. I was laid off in 1979 or 1980 due to budget cuts. I then went into private home nursing. After this, I went to work in nutrition in Pittsboro, North Carolina for four years. I then worked twenty hours a week at the Multi-Purpose Center. After this, I went to Home Health Nursing. I would still be doing this, but I was at a patient's house and fell down their steps and broke my hip, which ended my career forever. I am eighty-two years old now and most of the time I am confined to home because of the pain in my hip and back. I was sixty-three when this happened. These were some of the happiest days doing my job I really loved.

Doctors at the Haywood-Moncure clinic were: The late Dr. Samuel Putnam, Dr. Johnson, Dr. John Wasch, Dr. David McKaye, Dr. Ned Kelly, Dr. Jim Swankle (Pediatrics), Dr. Thomas Miller, Dr. Gallager, Dr. Hoole, Dr. Blomenthal, Dr. Thomas Wilson (Mental Health), Dr. Dingfeller ,and Dr. Ames. Counselor was Vivian Foushee. Secretaries were Mary Cross Seymore and Sandra Womble. Receptionist was the late Patricia Jones. Registration were: Geraldine Hayes and Stella Headen. Pharmacists were: Steve Almond, Rick Efird, and Mr. Lee. Pharmacy Technician was Edna Raines-McNeill. X-ray Technicians were: Irene Davis, Robena McCrimmon, and BJ Denton. Dentists were: Dr. Brooks, Dr. Campbell, and Dr. Love. FNPs were: Loretta Jean Dowdy, Ruth Efird, Ann-Marie Swankle (mid-wife), Marie Shirey, Jessie Goins, Allene Fuller, Deborah Freeman, and Hettie Negel. Project Director was Paul Alston. Moses Carey, Jr. was Director over all three clinics.

We had after school help from the students at Northwood High School. One of the ones I remember was Stevie Partin. He did various jobs, such as stocking supplies and cleaning up. Alean Brooks worked in the lab and clinic. Barbara Eaves worked in the clinic and registration. We had drivers: Geraldine Haynes, Oscar Cotton, Leroy Jacobs, and Percy Farrington. Levander Smith stocked rooms and cleaned. Wanda Glosson and Bill Harris were Unit Managers. Peggy Williams worked as a CHW for a short time and they worked in the clinic. Geneva Parker worked most of the time with the WIC program. There were several students from UNC-Chapel Hill that came and met with us CHWs to find out about the old time remedies and superstitions and about different treatments. This time was a lot of fun to me. I hay have forgotten someone or misspelled their names and I apologize for this. It was not intentional.

As submitted by Martha Lucille Holden

Rebecca T. Clegg, Community Health Worker

Between 1971 and 1972, I was approached about taking some training at the UNC Hospital for community health worker. We were taught to do social work, health care, work with alcoholics, and so many other things. I enjoyed it. I had to go to Chapel Hill every day for several weeks, and then we started the clinic at Moncure-Pittsboro road.

There was a long trailer with two big blocks at each corner. I'll never forget as we started out on the first day. I was given an orange colored bag, pencils, paper, and a note pad. Dr. Samuel Putnam was requesting that we see three to ten people per day, or recruit three to ten people per day. On my first day going put, I went to a little lady's house and I knocked on the door. She came to the door and I explained to her about the Health Center and the help she could get there. She said she didn't have any money or a way to get there (no transportation). I told her I thought we could work that out. I think she was the second or third patient to come into the center, and after she came in, there were five or six more from her family to come. She was a very close person to me. I loved all of my patients and I think they loved me too. There were a lot of things to happen during my work that was kind of scary, but I made it. I'll never forget one day, I can't tell it all, it's just too much. I went out to pick a lady up that morning. She had called me around 6:00 a.m. or 6:30 a.m. She said she was going to meet me at the road. It was a good distance from where she lived out to the highway, so I told her, "please do not do that, I'll pick you up after I get to the center." When I got to the center, I got the transportation that had a radio on it and I went for her. When I got there, I knocked on the door and she didn't answer. I started around to the side of the house and her son was coming up into the yard. I told him, "I can't get your mother to answer the door." He said he would go around to the back where he could get inside. I went to a window and saw her sitting in a chair. When the son came back to the door for me, we went into her room together and there she sat with her scarf and coat on, she had expired. This really did something to me because I loved that little lady. I called back to the center and Mary Seymore came out to be with me and it was something strange about it, I never remembered anything else about that, other than Mary coming out to be with me at the time.

I served the Deep River Road, Colon Road, Osgood Road, and Cumnock Road. In fact, I had the ten mile radius from Deep River into Lee County and I enjoyed it.

I'll never forget one day I made such a blunder. Dr. Putnam being so firm and just right in everything he did, sent me out to make a visit to check a lady. I went out and she was sitting in a chair looking kind of strange. Now of course I had never been around a diabetic and no knowing much about diabetes, I checked her blood pressure and as I came close to her, she had a sweet smell about her breath. After checking her blood pressure, it was not too good. I went back and told Dr. Putnam what I thought and my thinking was all wrong. Oh my goodness he just got on me. He called me Becky. He said, "Becky go back and get that lady," I jumped in the car and down the road I went. It was a small car and it was bouncing and bumping over the dirt roads. I got her and brought her into the center. Dr. Putnam sent her right on to the hospital. The lady was about to go into a diabetic coma. He was very firm and after that incident, I always listened to him very carefully and I knew he meant business and of course I wanted to do what was right. The diabetic patient went to the hospital and she got along fine. There were a lot of things that I ran into that were kind of scary because we worked with social parts of the patients with alcoholics and mental patients.

One day I went out to see a man. I did not know him very well because he had just come into the center. Of course that nurse practitioner who sent me there wanted me to check his blood pressure. I went out and he met me at the door in his BVDs. There was a chair right at the door and one at the end of the table. I thought it looked a little strange, even though he was nice. I said "sit down and let me check your blood pressure." I checked it right quick, and seeing and looking how I could get out of the door real quick, so I kindly backed out. I said "Mr. Joe, your blood pressure is up just a little bit. The nurses want me to go and check someone else's pressure right away, but I'll be back. I'll be in touch with you." I went right back to the Health Center and I told the nurse. "Ruthy" was my practitioner that I worked with. I told her how he was dressed, and she said "Oh, Rebecca I forgot to tell you that he was a little mental problem." He did not bother me, he didn't say anything out of the way and this went off very well. From then on she tried to tell me about the patients' needs.

There were so many things the Moncure Clinic was helping people who had not had any help in the past. One day, Dr. Putnam sent me out to check on a young girl. I cannot remember what type of problem she had, but she had some type of affliction that prevented her from working. He told me to go out and check on her and talk to her about Social Security. I did not know very much about it but I went on and thought, Lord help me. I talked to her and her mother said she did not get any social security. So then I told her what the doctor said. I did not know after that whether she had gotten help or not. Years later, I saw this lady in a store. She remembered me. But I did not remember her. I said, "I don't remember you," and she said, "I remember you." She spoke so friendly and kind. She said "you helped my daughter get social security." It was such a joy to know we were helping people at the center. I'll always remember Dr. Putnam as being a very kind person. He wanted us to do things that were right. I always thought the group was so wonderful to work with. Each community health worker was assigned to a nurse practitioner.

I do not think I had but one practitioner while I worked there and that was Ms. Ruth Efird. We got along well together. There was always happiness and joy with all the employees. This was one thing Dr. Putnam put emphasis on because I am sure that he knew we needed to love each other so that it would make us love those persons we went out to visit. There was always a smile and we always put forth an effort to go the extra mile with all of the people, and I think it was my gift that God was just a blessing to me because I met people. There's one thing about the workers and the patients that came into the center, no one knew about the others they were working with. We did not even tell our co-workers about our patients. Only Dr. Putnam or whatever doctor was working with you and that particular person and the nurse practitioner. That was it and it was such a joy for me. We had early child development, we were taught. I worked with the social worker and I'll never forget one time we had to go to court, and this young man that was our social worker, he had long legs and we often laughed about it after everything was over. We sat there and things did not go like we thought it was going to go for us. It seemed that his legs just kept growing put this was an experience for us. We were just there for that person and that person only, whatever their needs. Whatever went on it was kept confidential with us. Nobody knew about it. We didn't talk about it with anybody.

Another part of the things that I came in contact with, there were so many things, the Lord was always with me as I went about doing for others. With the alcoholic program, I'll never forget one day a call came in from Gene Horton, who was the alcoholic counselor, to go out and pick up one of his patients. Upon arriving at this person's home, I told someone to tell him to come out and they did. They brought him out and put him in the back seat behind me and I thought, oh, how I can make it by myself, but this I had to do. We learned to do whatever had to be done. He talked fine and one or two times he got off basis, but I made it to the center with him and Gene Horton got him out. Gene carried him to the hospital and I think he was really into it for a while. But when he came back Gene and I, several of the workers, and his parents, had a sobriety celebration for him. He was a very nice young man and he was just so wonderful after that. He came home and he had a garden and raised the largest tomatoes and cucumbers that I had ever seen. These are the things I can look back at and remember, and appreciate doing, even with fear sometimes but it always ended up with joy. Sometimes we would get involved in personal care. We would carry medicine to people who needed it, and sometimes we would have to pick them up because the transportation was in other areas. I'll never forget one day one of the other health workers asked me to go with her to visit patient who needed personal care, and it was so sad. This man, he was an older person, we had one of the male workers to go with us. During that time, men did not accept women giving them baths. It was so sad with him. So I went out and we bathed him. We had to change the water two or three times. We ran into a lot of situations that were so sad, but we did it with pride and joy, because those people needed help, and this is what we did.

As submitted by Rebecca Thompson Clegg

Edna R. McNeil - Pharmacy Technician

I began working at Haywood-Moncure Health Center in 1972. When I had my interview, I had to go before the board. I felt as if I was going to work for the Federal Bureau of Investigation. My job was as an Appointment Clerk. I not only scheduled appointment for our clinic, but did referrals for patients that needed more involved health care. We mainly sent patients to UNC Hospital in Chapel Hill, North Carolina. Working as an Appointment Clerk, I learned about different diseases.

We were a comprehensive health clinic. We had a Pharmacy Department, Dental Department, and Social Services Department. We also had Community Health Workers. They worked out in the field (the community). Most of our patients did not have regular medical check-ups, so the Moncure Clinic was very important to the community and the surrounding areas.

We had three clinics at the same time. The other medical centers were in Chapel Hill-Carrboro and Prospect Hill. As I continued to work at the Moncure site, I became interested in medicine. We had a small pharmacy at that time and only had one pharmacist and he worked part-time. So our patient load grew and the pharmacist was hired full-time, and needed someone to assist him. I became a pharmacy technician. I became a certified Pharmacy Technician at the School of Pharmacy in Chapel Hill, North Carolina.

Our patient load continued to grow. So we had to have a larger space. I enjoyed working at the Haywood-Moncure Health Center site. It was very rewarding. I learned a lot and enjoyed the relationship I had with the patients and staff.

As submitted by Edna Raines McNeill

Alean H. Brooks – Lab Technican

My name is Alean H. Brooks. I have been asked to give a written account of my thoughts and experiences as a clinical assistant at Haywood-Moncure Health Center.

Paul Alston was a compassionate and devoted leader of our community. His desire to build a health center that would provide affordable health care for all the citizens of Chatham County was a direct result of the tragic death of his father. He believed that if there had been a local health facility, his father might have lived.

While working at the Chatham County Health Department as a family planning coordinator, I heard about Paul Alston's vision to build a health center in Moncure. My supervisor, Elva Butler, helped me write my resume and I was hired as a clinical assistant. I was very excited about being a part of Paul Alston's vision. Paul was able to secure funds from the federal government for the Haywood-Moncure Health Center as well as health centers in Chapel Hill and Prospect Hill.

Because Haywood-Moncure Health Center was staffed with the doctors from NC Memorial Hospital, things were not always easy. The executives at the hospital liked Paul Alston's idea for a community health center; it seemed as though they wanted to wrestle the control from Paul. At a meeting with the North Carolina Memorial Hospital executives, they said they wanted to save the integrity of the Haywood-Moncure Health Center by going in a new direction. They said that the staff had to be more professional. It seemed as though NCMH executives were saying that we had to stop being friendly to our patients. In those days, I was either very brave or very foolish. I stood up in the meeting and told the NCMH executives that if they took the heart out of the health center, it would not be worth saving. I told them that you put stress on the staff; it would trickle down to the patients. Later, Paul Alston thanked me for my comments.

On another occasion, one of the doctors at Haywood-Moncure Health Center participated in a civil rights rally in Greensboro. Some of the protesters, including the doctor's fiancée, were killed by the KKK clansmen who broke up the rally. A petition was started to fire the doctor from the health center. Once again, I spoke out on behalf of the doctor, saying that the doctor should not be fired because she stood up for what she believed in. I told the head of the petition that she was a good doctor and that the health center needed her. Later, the petition was dropped. Paul Alston thanked me again.

As I look back on this particular incident; I have to wonder if I was very brave or very foolish. A co-worker and I went to the beauty salon one morning before going to work. While I was under the hair dryer, a man walked into the shop and demanded that we give him the keys to one of the cars in the parking lot. He had his back to me and I could see that he was holding a finger nail file pretending it was a knife. When I got home from under the dryer, I could see that the man was small and unsteady on his feet. I said to the hairdresser and my co-worker, "we can take him." So we pushed him against the couch, threw him off balance and turned him upside down. I was holding him up by his legs and feet. One of my friends was choking him and my other friend was looking for something to hit him with. She couldn't find anything so I told her to hit him in the private parts. When he heard what we were going to do to him, he really started kicking, fighting, and trying to get away from us. He finally ran out of the door in fear of his life. Later, the police told us he was an escaped convict. I had to be treated at the health center for some scratches from his finger nail file. I told my supervisor that we were late coming to work because we were held hostage in the beauty salon by an escaped convict.

As a clinical assistant at Haywood-Moncure Health Center, my job was to order supplies, stock the doctor's office, check in patients by taking their vital signs, draw their blood, and take urine samples. I also learned how to be specific when I gave a patient a cup and asked for a sample. One day, this particular patient gave me a sample alright, only it was a stool sample inside this little urine cup. Until this day, I do not know how the patient got that stool sample into that tiny cup! I was often cross-trained to do other jobs. When I learned to do electrocardiograms (EKGs), I was taught that if you run out of EKG paper don't panic and say *"Oh no!"* because your patient will sit up and say *"What is it, what's the matter, Am I going to die?"* Because I had experience doing x-rays at the Chatham County Health Department, I also volunteered to do x-rays because Haywood-Moncure Health Center did not have an X-ray technician. I soon discovered that with my regular duties as a clinical assistant, as well as the volunteer x-ray technician, I had a little too much on my plate.

Paul Alston and one of our first doctors, Dr. Sam Putman, taught the staff to be proud of Haywood-Moncure Health Center and to have love and respect for each other. Those expressions of love made the health center a warm and compassionate place for patients to receive the best health care. It seemed as though we did a lot of hugging and saying, *"I love you"*, which spilled over in our homes and family lives. Now, after all these years, I have turned into a big hugger and still hug my family members and others. I tell them *"I love you"* every chance I get.

Under Paul's leadership, Haywood-Moncure Health Center continued to flourish. It changed the quality of life for all its patients and staff. Thank you, Paul, Alston for your vision.

As submitted by Alean H. Brooks

Barbara Eaves – Clerical Intake Worker/Lab Technician

My tenure of employment with the Moncure Community Health Center was a unique time of experiences. I began working with the center in the year 1973 as a driver. I took an interest in helping in the clinic and later was titled as a Clinical Assistant. During the year 1984, I began having medical problems with standing. The Registration Clerk position became vacant. Some of my most loveable co-workers suggested I speak with Mr. Alston, Project Director, regarding the position. I was fortunate enough to obtain the position.

I enjoyed working with the patients and staff in all positions. My effort was to do what I could for whom I could when I could. I always enjoyed helping patients who were under financial pressure. I referred many patients who I thought would be eligible for help to the appropriate agency I felt would give them assistance.

I remember one man that was receiving his monthly Social Security check at a minimal amount. I suggested he go back to the Social Security Administration and inquire to apply for Supplementary Income. The next time I saw the man, he was happy. I wish I could have recorded his emotional and verbal reactions. This story is one of the many I encountered during my position as Registration Clerk.

I am glad the Moncure Health Center is still in existence. There are many people that need the type of services they offer and to remind you I myself continue to receive my primary health care at the Moncure Health Center.

As submitted by Barbara Eaves

Helen S. Farrar – Medical Records Clerk

I was excited to be one of the applicants hired in that day in 1972. Working in health care was new to me. I came to Orange-Chatham Comprehensive Health Services, Inc. from the Sanford School System as a teacher's aide.

Our orientation was done at the Haywood-Moncure Multi-Purpose Center. Our interviewing and training was done in Chapel Hill on Rosemary Street in the conference room.

Haywood-Moncure Health Center was opened on April 15, 1972; we helped with bringing in furniture and setting up files. Sandra Hart and I worked in medical records. Sandra did transcription and I managed the files. Our supervisor was Shirley Harris; John Holland was the Unit Manager.

The center began with just four trailers, but grew very rapidly. Our services included: medical, dental, mental health, x-ray, nutrition, optometry, pharmacy, transportation, WIC, and social services.

I, along with most of my family received my medical care at Haywood-Moncure. Dr. Samuel Putnam, one of our first physicians was very caring and unique, to say the least, but we all loved him. He would have us hug each other at the end of our weekly staff meetings, especially if there were disagreements. He planted a pecan tree in front of the center's entranceway that is still standing today.

We had a yard beautification project in later years, as our staff and community came out on a Saturday to set out many azaleas. We took great pride in our health center, and patients received good care. We worked hard, but we were able to enjoy each other.

Since we were partially funded by the federal government, each year at grant time, we became concerned and anxious about our funding for the next year. Congressman David Price was recognized as being a great help to us in this area. Personnel came and went, but the sincere concern and commitment for the patients did not change. I feel privileged to have worked with a special group of people and for the training experience.

A year or two before I left OCCHS, there were cut backs. There were fears, a feeling of uncertainty and suspicion. The staff's morale was very low. There was a short setback for the clinic.

Mr. Paul Alston had a vision for those unable to obtain health care because of cost and availability. His vision became a reality. For this we are grateful.

As submitted by Helen S. Farrar

Sandra H. Void – Medical Transcriptionist

I can remember interviewing for the position of the office clerk at the Orange Chatham Comprehensive Health Center in March, 1972. I interviewed with Dr. Samuel Putnam, the Medical Director. My primary duties were serving as switchboard operator and providing transcription duties for clinic notes and file management. I worked from March 1972 until March 1973 when I moved away due to marriage.

My office was located where I could see all that entered the facility and it was a family atmosphere. I became not just a co-worker but a friend to those that I worked with on a daily basis. My closest working relationship was with Helen Heck because we shared an office and learned from each other. I also remember working with Jean Dowdy who was an FNP and Ruth Efird, Mary Headen, a Van Driver, Mary Cross, and the staff that went out into the community was community people who were well received.

We were a service-oriented facility with a family atmosphere. The staff was so nice to me when I submitted my resignation due to my pending marriage. They gave me a surprise bridal shower at the home of Jean Dowdy and everyone attended. The older ladies would share their personal marriage tips with me.

One of my tasks included traveling to Prospect Hill on an as-needed basis to provide transcription services. I received a very supportive letters of recommendation from Dr. Sam Putnam which I continue to use even today as I continue my professional career.

My current position is that of Administrative Office II at UNC School of Medicine in Medical Science teaching Labs. I serve as budget manager and human resources facilitator. I will always cherish the memories I have from working at the Moncure Health Center.

As submitted by Sandra Hart Void

Levander Smith - Custodian

Levander Smith has been the custodian at Moncure-Haywood Health Center almost since its opening

He has worked very hard to keep the health center and grounds clean and neat.

He is responsible for opening and closing the center every day it is operational. When the security system goes off Mr. Smith would be there. Levander, an employee who is trustworthy, faithful, dependable highly motivated, significant to the Moncure-Haywood Health Center.

As submitted by Jean Dowdy, RN, FNPC, BA

Faye Schulz – Medical Transcriptionist

My name is Faye Schulz and I worked with the Orange Chatham Comprehensive Health, Moncure Health Center for approximately six years from 1974 - 1979.

My experience working at the center was remarkable. The staff was very professional and also fun.

The memories I have of each person I will cherish forever. Moncure was like a family that I will never forget.

I started as a Medical Transcriptionist. I taught medical terminology at Central Carolina Community College. My careers range from Office Nurse to Independent Contractor to owning Mrs. Lacy's Magnolia House in Sanford, North Carolina.

As submitted by Faye Schulz

A Plan for Medical Services at
Orange-Chatham Comprehensive Health Services, Inc.

Submitted

May 17, 1976

Max Michael, M.D. - Medical Director
Primary Care
(July 1, 1976)

and

Gay Kayye, R.N.., F.N.P.
Nursing Director

"It is essential for the stability and efficient functioning of the body social that each of its sub-divisions should operate as an autonomous, self-reliant unit which, though subject to control from above, must have a degree of independence and take routine contingencies in its stride, without asking higher authority for instructions."

~Arthur Koestler

The Ghost in the Machi

CONTENTS

INTRODUCTION

Jean Dowdy~Marjorie Land~Glenda Hargraves

Orange-Chatham Comprehensive Health Services, Inc.

105 Roberson Street

Carrboro, North Carolina 27510
May 17, 1976

To the Staff of Orange-Chatham Comprehensive Health Services, Inc.

This plan for medical services within OCCHS is submitted because of an expressed need for goals and priorities. Too much of what happens appears haphazard or the result of rapid decisions in reaction to situations. The consequences of these processes are often a combination of confusion and frustration among the staff. Although the realities of OCCHS will continue to require rapid decisions, defined goals for the medical program are necessary if progress is to be achieved.

What we submit after six months of discussions is our perception about goals and begins to set priorities for the program. These suggestions clearly define our view of the program's mission, and as such are subject to bias in need of open discourse within all parts of the system.

We hope by submitting our plans to general scrutiny at least one month prior to the installation of a new medical director, everyone will have ample opportunity to comment.. We want the medical program not only to be unique, but also the result of a collective effort. We remain open for comments, objections, and suggestions.

We respectively submit this plan to the staff and administration on this
seventeenth day of May, 1976.
MAX MICHAEL, M.D.
GAY J. KAYYE, R.N.

1. A Policy Statement

The medical program of the Orange-Chatham Comprehensive Health Services is established with a single objective; the provision of medical services, primarily health and illness care to a target population on a continuous, comprehensive basis.

Continuous services are available and accessible twenty-four hours per day, three hundred and sixty-five says per year.

Comprehensive service is that combination of services within the overall medical program that includes mental health consultation, pharmaceutical services, social service, emergency services, nutritional **education, outreach programs, as well as full medical care services.** Though the contingencies of the funding process may alter the mix of these services, the provision and promotion of health is recognized as the primary goal of this medical program.

Furthermore, the Family Nurse Practitioner is the primary provider of medical care, participating in a team approach to primary care. Validation of this model is crucial to the medical program.

Finally, the autonomy of each center—Prospect Hill, Chapel Hill-Carrboro, and Haywood-Moncure—is completely recognized. Although a unified approach to the distribution of health services within the whole program is desirable the popularities of each community must remain of paramount consideration. Necessary program-wide policies reflect the broader needs for compliance with federal regulations, while suggested plans reflect the drive toward a high quality, innovative program. To each center equal time and effort must be devoted by the medical component administrator.

2. The Health Team Concept

The efforts in some neighborhood health centers toward developing a health team reflect several forces. First, there is a movement away from a competitive, hierarchal approach to medicine toward one of general cooperation. Second, the social and medical implications of an illness episode often require more expertise than a physician can be expected to have. And third, paraprofessionals and consumers realize the limitations of the physician as a sovereign decision maker. Regardless if the intuitive rationale a team approach makes, these new models are not without problems. In their book *Making Health Teams Work,* Wise and Beckhard describe some of these problems, such as role definitions and inter-team relationships. There is a necessary time commitment from all team members if the team is to function and serve as a source of improved care.

The health team concept has been a part if OCCHS since its inception. **Figure 1** shows the organizational structure of the program with its three basic "teams." Although this structure does not exactly conform to that discussed by Wise and Beckhard, the more informal team structure within the does appear to coincide more with this ideal.

Certainly the health team concept is logical for OCCHS with present staffing patterns. We suggest an active attempt to define functioning teams in each center. However, since the development of health teams is time consuming, staff meetings should be devoted to this developmental process on a regular basis. A possible structure is shown in **figure** 2, from the Wise and Beckhard's book, *Making Health Teams Work,* can serve as a fruitful guide and is available upon request.

Organizational Structure

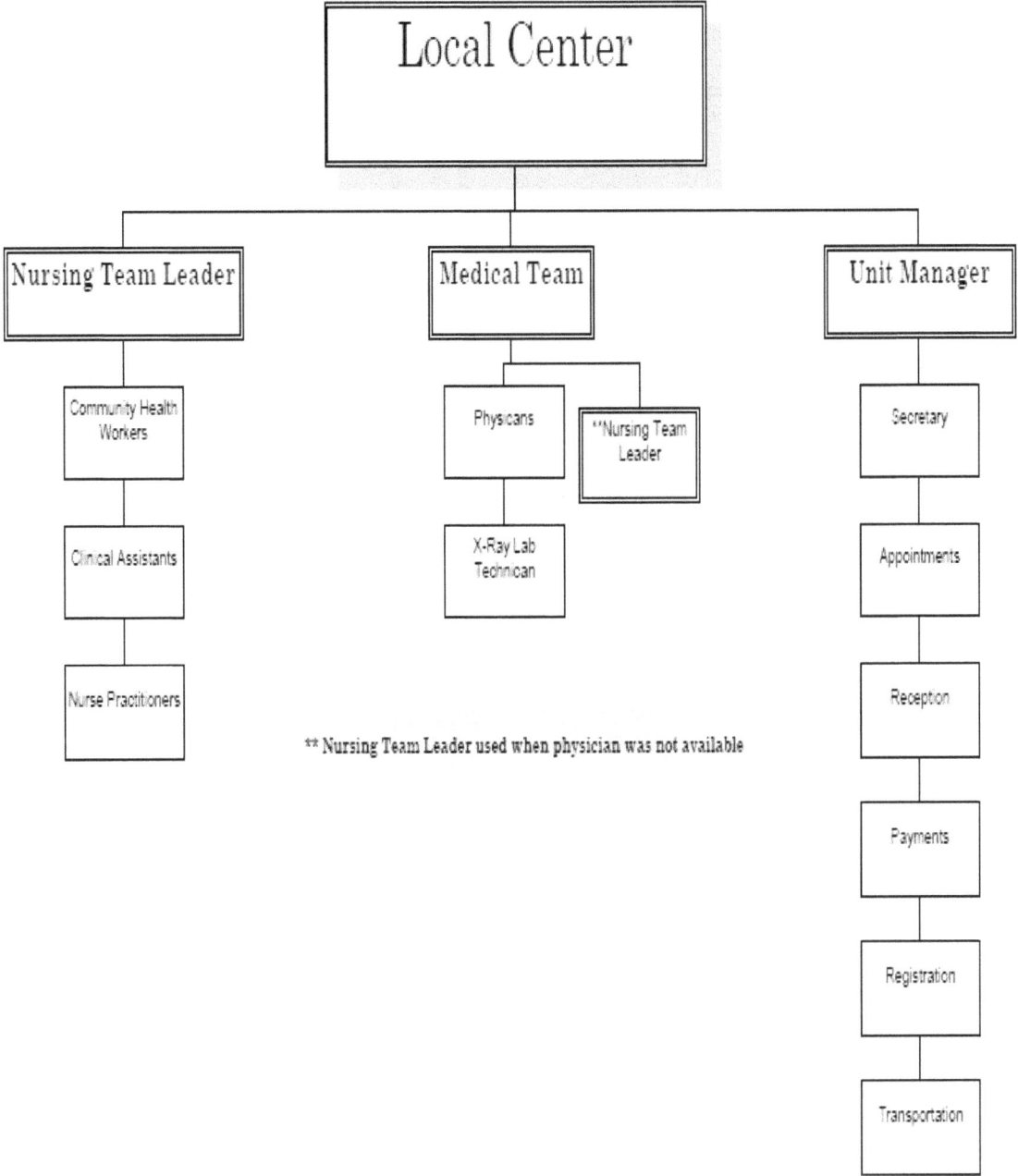

Figure 1:Organizational Structure

Health Team Structure

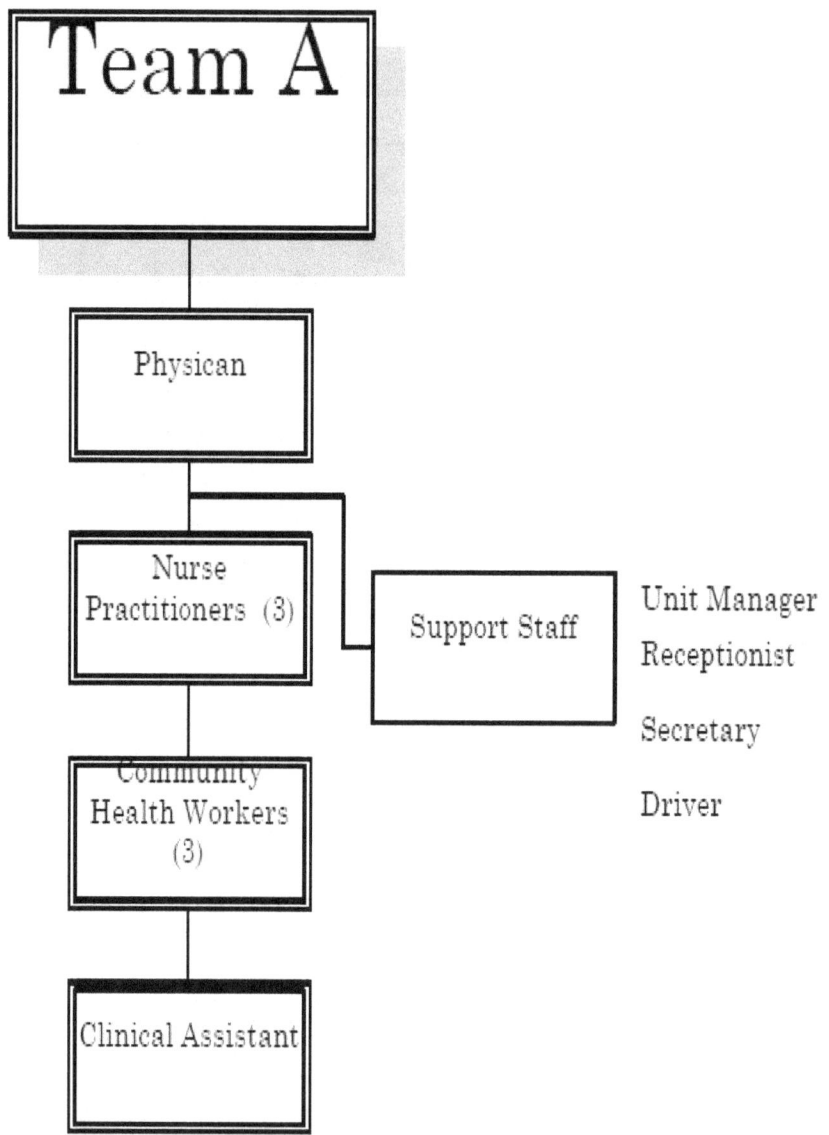

Figure 2: Health Team Structure

3. Family Nurse Practitioner Clinical Evaluation

The need for evaluation in all areas of health care is becoming increasingly recognized. No particular provider-type of specific delivery is immune from this need. However, since the Family Nurse Practitioner as well as other newly defined primary care providers are the most recent additions to the medical profession, it is not unreasonable to assume that these persons will be the first to have minimal evaluative criteria established by regulatory bodies for certification and recertification. In order to anticipate this type of process and recognizing the profound need to assure the clinical competence of the nurse practitioners, an organized program of clinical evaluation for the Family Nurse Practitioners is suggested.

The clinical evaluation should be approached by two methods. First, each FNP should have periodic written evaluation from each of the major clinical consultants. A suggested form is attached which permits the objectification of ten areas of clinical skill, plus ample area for additional comments. This form should be completed at least three times per year. Second, periodic observation of clinical competence should be instituted. Several approaches to this are available including a two-way mirror, direct observation during an encounter, and random checks on certain physical examination findings.

None of these approaches are without problems and limitations. We suggest that by October 1976 an operational program of clinical evaluation for the FNP be started. A work committee representative of FNP's and MD's will be established with the task of establishing criteria and methods for clinical evaluation. The full resources of the medical center, in particular the School of Nursing, and the medical literature should be used to meet these goals.

ORANGE CHATHAM COMPREHENSIVE HEALTH SERVICES, INC.
Family Nurse Practitioner Clinical Evaluation Form

Nurse Practitioner:

Evaluation: Date:_____

        5 – Excellent – clearly outstanding

        4 – Good – goes beyond mere performance of required

        3 – Fair or Satisfactory – adequate

        2 – Marginal – in need of remedial help

        1 – Unsatisfactory – inadequate

        0 – Insufficient information to evaluate

1. INFORMATION GATHERING. Ability and skilled in compiling a patient history and other information for diagnosis.

    0   1   2   3   4   5

Comment:

2. PHYSICAL EXAMATION. Ability and skilled in performing a physical examination.

    0   1   2   3   4   5

Comment:

3. PROBLEM SOLVING. Ability and skilled in using information gathered to develop a diagnosis and treatment plan.

    0   1   2   3   4   5

Comment:

4. CLINICAL JUDGMENT. Ability to use sound judgment in planning for and carrying out treatment.

    0   1   2   3   4   5

Comment:

5. **RELATING TO PATIENT.** Effectiveness in working with patients.

    0   1   2   3   4   5

Comment:

6. **LONG TERM RESPONSIBILITY.** Willingness to accept responsibility for continuing care.

    0   1   2   3   4   5

Comment:

7. **RELATING TO COLLEAGUES.** Ability to work effectively with colleagues and other members of the health team.

    0   1   2   3   4   5

Comment:

8. **RELIABILITY AND DEPENDAZBILITY.** Assumption of responsibility and extent to which practitioner can be trusted.

    0   1   2   3   4   5

Comment:

9. **FUND OF KNOWLEDGE.** Overall medical knowledge relevant to FNP practice.

    0   1   2   3   4   5

Comment:

10. **OVERALL COMPETENCE.** Overall competence taking into consideration all of the above.

    0   1   2   3   4   5

Comment:

Figure 3: Family Nurse Practitioner Clinical Evaluation Form

4. Community Health Worker

The concept of an outreach health worker has been part of the neighborhood health center movement since the late 1960's. Generally based upon an idea generated during the development of the Martin Luther King Health Center in New York, the community health worker model has seen a number of changes, fluctuations, and frustrations. Role definitions have been made ambiguous from the outset and have indeed remained a major impediment to the adoption of a consistent community health worker model or of methods to evaluate the efficacy of this relatively new health professional

OCCHS adopted the concept of the community health worker, although failed to define the position vis-à-vis the delivery of medical care. People from the community serve as liaison between the health centers and the community, yet remain in the often conflicting roles as advocates for the health center and for the community.

The experience from each center has been different. On the one hand the community health workers provide a valuable resource if information about patients to the center and vice versa, not to mention an invaluable role in patient care. However, on the other hand, some community health workers operate in vacuum without proper supervision or full utilization. Such divergent problems are not peculiar to OCCHS; they reflect the experiences nationwide.

In addition to the issues of role definition there is little data about the community health worker. Although we may intuitively assess their effects as beneficial, viability of the model depends upon documentation. These problems must be dealt with for several reasons:

> 1.Continued funding of the job will depend upon proven beneficial efficacy.

> 2.Support within each center hinges upon clear role definitions.

3.Defunding prospects raise the spectre of losing a developed community health worker model without understanding the implications of the model.

4.Without proper delineation of the model it cannot be positively altered.

To properly approach these problems an effort between the community health workers and medical providers is necessary.

First, each center should adopt a schedule of meetings between the community health workers and the providers at least three times per week. A simple record if these meetings should be kept to include the names of those present and in particular patients discussed and recommendations.

Second, an evaluation of what in particular the community health workers are doing should be started by August 1976. Such an evaluation should consist of a simple contact sheet (see attached) evaluated each week with a provider.

Third, assessment of the health worker's role should be judged every three months by the providers in an effort to determine the precise contribution to the health team made by these people. Procedures for this evaluation should be developed by providers and health workers.

Fourth, a program of continuing education should be established as soon as possible.

Jean Dowdy~Marjorie Land~Glenda Hargraves

COMMUNITY HEALTH WORKER CONTACT SHEET

Community Health Worker:

_____ *Date:* _____

Patient Name and Unit Number	Reason for Contact	Observations	What You Did	Follow-up	Providers

Figure 4: Community Health Worker Contact Sheet

132

5. Clinical Competence and Peer Review for Physicians

While the need for clinical evaluation of the nurse practitioners has been an implicit part of OCCHS since adopting this practice model, the program has been lacking in its efforts to establish comparable criteria for physicians. The reasons for the separate approach to the FNP and physician vis-à-vis clinical competence are easily found in the history of the paraprofessional movement and of Professional Standards Review Organizations development. Each movement has seemingly developed in parallel over the past decade. If OCCHS is to adopt criteria for the ongoing clinical evaluation of the FNP, similar criteria should be designed for the physicians. Clearly such a proposal is laden with emotional and methodological issues. These include physician autonomy, clinical authority, and actual standards of competence. Each should be fairly dealt with by the physicians while suitable methods of peer review are developed.

Several approaches are suggested. First, the medical audit is a method of clinical evaluation and perhaps a separate, periodic audit of physician charts should be undertaken to insure adequate constant review. Second, the requirements for continuing education are directed toward clinical competence. Third, each physician should be critically evaluated three or four times per year by the FNP's practicing with that physician. A suggested form is attached. Finally, and most difficult, is peer review by the physicians themselves. The methods include chart reviews, chart conferences, and problem solving conference. For each of these methods rudimentary designs are available.

A Peer Review Committee should be established by August 1, 1976 with the task of defining methods of peer review for OCCHS. At least one physician from each center should be represented and certainly all can participate. A report of suggestions should be completed by October 1, 1976, with plans for instituting peer reviews by November 1, 1976.

ORANGE CHATHAM COMPREHENSIVE HEALTH SERVICES, INC.
Physician Clinical Evaluation

Physician:

Evaluator: Date: _____

> 5 — Excellent — clearly outstanding
> 4 — Good — goes beyond mere performance of required
> 3 — Fair or Satisfactory — adequate
> 2 — Marginal — in need of remedial help
> 1 — Unsatisfactory — inadequate
> 0 — Insufficient information to evaluate

1. **CONSULTATIONS.** Ability and skilled in compiling a patient history and other information for diagnosis.

   0   1   2   3   4   5

   Comment:

2. **PHYSICAL EXAMATION.** Ability and skilled in performing a physical examination.

   0   1   2   3   4   5

   Comment:

3. **TEACHING.** Ability and skilled in using information gathered to develop a diagnosis and treatment plan.

   0   1   2   3   4   5

   Comment:

4. **RELATING TO COLLEAGUES.** Ability to use sound judgment in planning for and carrying out treatment.

   0   1   2   3   4   5

   Comment:

Figure 5: Physician Clinical Evaluation

6. Medical Audit

The process of medical audit has received a good deal of attention, most directed toward the issues of quality of medical care. To date, adequate methods of assessing are made that assurance if content within the medical record will in turn have a positive effect on quality. Regardless of the validity of this assumption, it is clear that the content analysis should continue on a regular process in OCCHS.

An additional method of content analysis is through criteria mapping, which focuses on a single tracer condition. Maps are currently under development in several major medical centers, in particular UCLA. A criteria map for Diabetes Mellitus is available and will require only minor modification for use in OCCHS. Such maps permit abstraction of a chart in 20-25 minutes.

This method of medical audit should be explored, in addition to efforts at further refinements of the present protocols, including careful documentation of the audit. Furthermore, a "Quality of Medical Care" file will be started immediately to provide the practice with a complete literature base from which to begin establishing methods of quality assurance within OCCHS.

7. Continuing Education

The growing emphasis of the medical profession on the establishment of criteria for continuing education reflects the demands for standards of recertification and a desire to assure quality of care. OCCHS should establish similar criteria and standards for its providers. Such an effort is clearly in advance of eventual regulations currently under study by state professional societies for licensure requirements.

Setting and maintaining criteria for continuing education serves to insure that each provider is knowledgeable of the current state of the art in medicine and is making an ongoing effort to continue the educational process. By anticipating recertification requirements, the continuing education program within OCCHS should establish individual patterns of education that will make the transition to the eventual regulations easier. Hopefully, the efforts on the part of the individual provider and OCCHS will in turn improve the quality of care within the clinic network.

The best available models for criteria if continuing education are those established by the American Medical Association for the Physician's Recognition Award and the Continuing Education Recognition Program if the North Carolina Nurses Association. The AMA criteria have been adopted by several state medical societies as criteria fir recertification. These stats include California, Arizona, Oregon, Maryland, New Mexico, and North Carolina. These criteria with only the modifications of hours requirements should be adopted for physicians employed full time by OCCHS. The slight modifications listed below for the Family Nurse Practitioners are derived more from the AMA standards because of the role of the FNP as a primary care provider.

In addition to the criteria listed below, each center should have funds made available for the establishment of library. This should include a reasonable selection of general medical journals and recent textbooks.

Physicians

> **Category I:** At least 30 hours per year of continuing education earned through attendance at programs sponsored by accredited organizations as defined by the AMA; e.g. UNC Grand Rounds
>
> **Category II**: No more than 10 hours per year for activities related to journal club presentations, teaching sessions, and the like given at OCCHS. (Non-accredited sponsorship)
>
> **Category III:** No more than 10 hours per year for publications or

presentations. Five hours credit given for each paper, etc.

Category IV: No more than 25 hours per year for non-supervised individual activities including self-instruction, consultation, patient care review, self-assessment examinations, and preparation for specialty boards.

Category V: No more than 10 hours per year for activities deemed applicable by the provider but not included in other categories.

TOTAL REQUIRED: 60 hours per year

Family Nurse Practitioners

Category I: At least 20 hours per year continuing education earned through attendance at national, regional, or local (including OCCHS) programs.

Category II: No more than but at least 6 hours per year for activities related to journal club presentations for teaching sessions to other providers.

Category III: No more than 10 hours per year for publications or presentations. Five hours credit given for each paper, etc.

Category IV: No more than 0 hours per year for non-supervised individual activities including self-instruction, consultation, patient care review, self-assessment examinations, and preparation for specialty boards.

Category V: No more than 8 hours per year for activities deemed applicable by the provider but not included in other categories.

TOTAL REQUIRED: 45 hours per year.

A file will be maintained and it is the responsibility if each provider to regularly record continuing education activities completed in each category.

The recording year begins January 1 with the presentation of a certificate of continuing education upon the completion of criteria.

Persons failing to meet the established criteria must fulfill the criteria by February 15th every year if appropriate disciplinary actions are to be avoided.

8. Conference Schedules

Since the primary mission of OCCHS is the provision of health care to a target population, the development of health teams and continuing education should be accomplished around the demands of patient care. As providers of health services, the nurse practitioners and physicians must recognize the need to maximize the quality of patient contact during the usual work week. The schedule outlined below is a suggested routine that allows for adequate team conferences and continuing education. The two hours per week can be altered in a variety of ways depending upon the desires of the local center, and indeed even increased. In addition, provision is made for charting and ongoing interaction between the providers and the community health workers.

1. Continuing education should be scheduled for one hour per week, example, between 8:30 a.m. and 9:30 p.m. Each four hours per month is divided between internal medicine, pediatrics, and obstetrics, with other relevant topics included as necessary be . The programs are the joint responsibility of the physicians and nurse practitioners.

2. Team conferences should be held one hour per week, example, between 9:30 a.m. and 10:30 a.m. the same day continuing education is held. Responsibility for establishing a meeting schedule for these sessions resides with the Unit Manager; although each meeting should be led by a different team member.

3. Community health worker conferences should be held each of the other

four days during the week. At least 30 minutes should be devoted to an ongoing assessment of patient needs, questions from the health workers, and general business pertaining to this part of the program. Each provider should be present at least three times per week to insure adequate follow-up on problems the community health workers' have with individual patients. A list of providers who will be present on a particular day is the responsibility of the Triad in each center.

4. The FNP meeting on the third Thursday of each month should no longer be held after August 1976 because of mixed reactions to these sessions and poor attendance. One lunch hour per month will be scheduled at the local centers with the Nursing and/or Medical Directors to discuss problems, etc. If longer sessions are necessary, a dinner will be scheduled, particularly if the entire program feels the need to gather to discuss issues.

5. The use of the Home Visit half-day remains controversial. As presently constituted, this time is being utilized for catching up on chart dictation plus an occasional home visit. To better utilize this time, home visits should be scheduled and documented for adequate review. Chart dictation remains a part of the usual routine and should be done immediately after a visit, not during home visits days. The majority of home visit duties can probably be handled by the Community Health Workers and discuss the daily meetings.

6. To insure adequate time during the week to sign charts, providers should schedule 30 minutes each day for this purpose.

9. Practice Schedules

As presently practiced at OCCHS, medical care is a convenient 9-5 proposition: an easy routine allowing the system to take off the "cream." During off hours this results in completely inadequate care, particularly as most patients wind up in a local Emergency Room (NCMH or Siler City) where care is notoriously poor or the physicians are unaware of a particular patient's problems. To change this inadequate way medicine is practiced within the centers, a twenty-four, comprehensive practice model should be adopted.

It is recognized that the committee surrounding the Haywood-Moncure and Prospect Hill centers may be over utilizing on-call services at present and should not participate in a more comprehensive practice model during the first phase. Instead, solutions to these problems should be sought, particularly through a process of community education about the use of emergency services. This effort can be carried out through the community health workers plus local advertising (see Marketing). During the efforts in Chapel Hill, the other centers will maintain the usual practice schedule, but will have only two sets of providers for cross coverage instead of the usual three.

The Chapel Hill center should initiate a twenty-four practice model beginning September 1, 1976 and extending for five months as an evaluation period. Prior to the initiation of this effort records should be kept by providers in Chapel Hill center and in the NCMH ER about the number and kind of contacts during July and August. The plan as outlined below should be viewed as a model in need of careful evaluation and testing.

1. First call rotated by nurse practitioners and will extend from 8:00 p.m. to 8:00 a.m. With six FNP's in Chapel Hill this means one night call every sixth day.

2. Second call will be a physician, with a physician being available every night.

3. The nurse practitioner covering during the night will not be scheduled

   for patient care the next day from 8:30 a.m. until 1:30 p.m.; patient responsibilities resume at 1:30 p.m.

4. Every effort will be made to absolutely avoid house calls unless medically necessary. The Orange County Rescue Squad should be utilized to transport patients to the center (provider on call have keys) and then to the ER if necessary.

5. If a physician evaluation on call before the patient is sent to the ER.

6. If a visit to the ER is necessary, a complete record will be sent the patient.

7. Results of any ER visits will be determined in the morning.

8. A separate set of charges will be established for these procedures, some of which must include case.

9. Hospital rounds on Chapel Hill patients will be scheduled each day to insure continuity of care. The provider usually responsible for a particular patient should make every effort to participate in these rounds; however, it is recognized this may not always be feasible.

10. Laboratory Practices

Laboratory tests constitute a major expenditure within the OCCHS system. Approximately $140,000 is allocated for the current fiscal year to cover tests performed by Biomedical Laboratories and through the central laboratories at NCMH. The approximate costs for these services appear in **table 1.** Because of these costs a major change in the provision of laboratory services is necessary if this part of the program is to remain viable,

An additional impetus for change is the pending legislation in the United States. Congress. Senate Bill S.1737 (Javitts-Kennedy) entitled "Clinical Laboratory Improvement Act of 1975," and House Bill H.R. 11341 (Rogers) entitled "Clinical Laboratory Improvement Act of 1976," are presently under construction and would establish strict requirements for laboratory testing and personnel. These regulations would serve to eliminate in part the role of the Clinical Assistants as described in the three centers. In addition, re-education and certification of the Clinical Assistants to a level meeting federal guidelines (Clinical Laboratory Assistant) appear currently unrealistic.

From this information it would seem reasonable to assume that the laboratory services at OCCHS are in need of a fundamental organizational change. As shown in **figure 7** the suggested reorganization of the labs. A registered laboratory technician should be hired as a coordinator of lab services for the program. The major feature of these services would be a central lab located at the Carrboro facility until the feasibility of this approach is defined. Besides being responsible for the tests listed in **table 2**, this person would also supervise quality control of the Clinical Assistants in Haywood-Moncure and in Prospect Hill. A quality control can be coordinated through NCMH and the College of American Pathologists' program. All other tasks performed by the C.A.'s will come under the purview of the local triad,

Table II details the number and type of tests performed currently by Biomedical Laboratory along with the projected costs for a single year. A laboratory technician performing the tests listed in **table 1** could realize a reduction in payments to Biomedical Laboratory from $65,000 to $122,000 per year. The additional $57,000 would easily provide capital for the new position, supplies, and back-up services at NCMH. Furthermore, monies not presently collected for tests perfumed would not have such a heavy financial burden upon the clinic and indeed the lab could become a source of additional revenue within the system.

Although not directly assessed in this section, additional savings can probably be realized by having physicians within the centers (or in a central location) read all the Electrocardiograms except in Chapel Hill. X-rays could probably be red at the reduced cost by hiring a part-time radiologist for this purpose. Both of these avenues of cost accounting need to be explored.

It is proposed that such a system of lab services be adopted on a trial basis within OCCHS by August 1, 1976 for six months. During this time, careful evaluation of this proposal could continue to determine the feasibility of extending the service to each center.

Proposed Organizational Structure of Laboratory Services

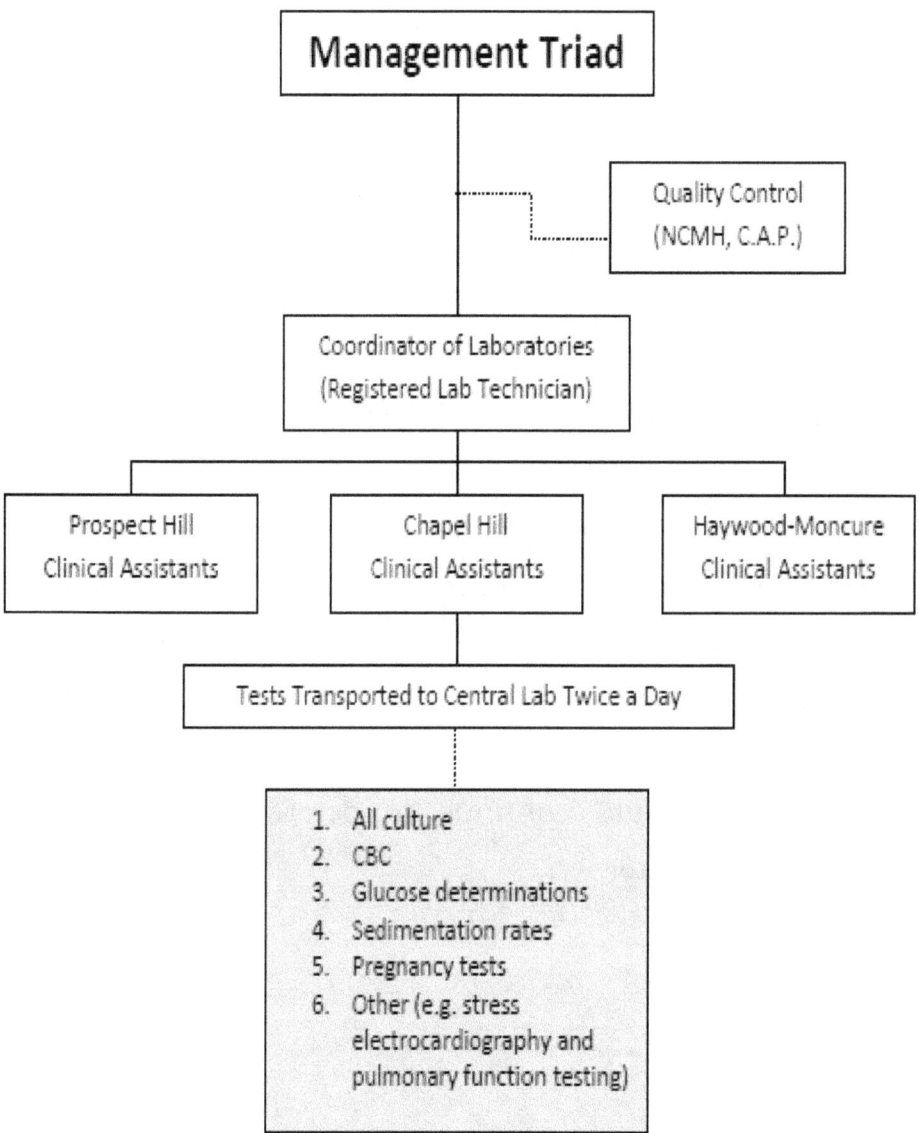

Figure 6: Organizational Structure of Laboratory Services

Costs of Laboratory Services			
	Chapel Hill	**Prospect Hill**	**Haywood-Moncure**
NCMH and Biomedical	$39,667	$39,667	$39,667
Dental Labs	$6,800	$6,800	$6,800
Specialty Clinics	$8,500	$8,500	$8,500
Reserve	$10,00	$10,000	$10,000

Table 1: Cost of Laboratory Services

Laboratory Tests			
Test	No. per month	Cost per month/ per center	Cost per month/ per OCCHS
Throat culture	67	$333	$1,000
Urine culture	53	$427	$1,280
OC culture	24	$195	$584
Wound culture	4	$32	$96
Glucose	16	$32	$96
CBC	267	$534	$1,603
Biochemistries	334	$2,338	$7,014
RPR	17	$34	$102

Table 2: Laboratory Tests

Note: This data represents an average of four months experience at the Chapel Hill Center. Total cost to the program is $122,064.00.

11. Systems Approach to Health Services Problems

Systems analysis is a method of studying a problem in a logical manner, viewing it in the context of the whole of which it is a part. It involves the identification first of the problem, second, of the objectives involved in solving the problem, third the breakdown of the problem into its component parts, and fourth the presentation of solutions based on the data that has been gathered.

This approach has significant potential for some of the generic bureaucratic problems encountered within OCCHS, such as the volume of paperwork, practice schedules, and patient flow. The latter problem was the focus of some informal observations made at the Chapel Hill-Carrboro center in September 1975. Results of these obser4vations are presented here to exemplify the process of a system view of patient flow, and one of many possible solutions.

Figure 9 diagram the flow of a patient during a typical visit. A total of 11 separate stops is not at all unusual. Figure 2 shows the flow of an FNP during a typical encounter. There is wasted movement that creates inefficiency, delays, and frustration.

If it is assumed that the function of the center is the provisional health care, then the form of the structure should conform to that function. Such an ideal reflects the dictum of art and architecture: Form Follows function. The building should have an interior design that permits the most efficient, effective functioning as a health center. Clearly, it does not presently have such a design.

By viewing first the function of the health center and then designing its form, the problem of patient flow (at the least) is solved. Figure 3 shows one possible suggested change in the partitioning of the center that reduces wasted motion by patient, provider, and support staff. A system approach to problems in all centers can be valuable and should be explored, especially as Haywood-Moncure moves toward building a new facility and prospect Hill additional temporary space.

12. Marketing

A source of concern within the program is a growing patient population. Probably the result of a multiplicity of causes, a static patient base is detrimental to a morale and may raise questions about the viability of the program.

For example, with a population of 40,000 in the township, the Chapel Hill center should be able to generate a large patient volume. This is particularly relevant when one considers the catchment area is larger than the township. Two problems contribute to this problem.

First, the program started as an OEO funded project with all the attendant restrictions and perceptions by the target population. With a change in funding, the mission of OCCHS has also changed somewhat, now seeking to provide services to anyone who desires the services. However, the people in Chapel Hill do not really know about this change of image.

Second, too few people are aware of the available services. Although there remains a modest amount of competition for patients in the area, a large number of people could be drawn to the program.

Similar sets of circumstances may exist in the other centers, although the particular problems in trying to attract a larger patient base may be different. In general, however, there is a lack of dissemination of information about the program into the community. Several approaches to this issue are suggested below and must be expanded. The basic source of information for a marketing approach comes from Kotler's <u>Marketing for Nonprofit Organizations.</u>

1. Use Community health workers to present households a package explaining services

2. Radio and newspaper stories focused on the role of the community health worker, the FNP, sickle screen, etc.

3. TV spot announcements.

4. Market analysis.

5. Publication of fee schedule.

6. Development of new programs (see Promotive Health Assessment).

13. Promotive Health Assessment Program

1. Introduction

Despite the continued expansion of medical technology and manpower there have been few changes in morbidity and mortality figures reflecting a general improvement in health status. Life expectancy remains essentially static regardless of the recent advances in various medical interventions including drugs, surgery, diagnostics hardware, And life support systems. Indeed, the apparent inability of a "moon-shot approach" to provide solutions of medicine. The promises of medicine's golden age beginning with the discovery of antibiotics have not been realized.

Tuberculosis is a disease of industrialization. During the 19th century, tuberculosis was the major cause of death among adults. Although there were some changes in tuberculosis mortality during the late 19th and early 20th centuries, a potent weapon against the disease was unavailable until the discovery of antibiotics. These "silver bullets" promised the eradication of the disease in this country. As the realization of that promise seemed imminent and certainly obtainable. However, if the history of tuberculosis is examined closely, it is apparent that the slope of the decline is prevalence has remained unchanged from 1850 to the present. The introduction of the sulfas, penicillin, streptomycin, and finally isoniazid did not change an already rapidly declining prevalence. Instead of medical science being responsible for the gradual disappearance of tuberculosis in this country, credit must be given to several factors including changes in sanitation, housing, nutrition, and host immunity.

Medical science can claim with ample justification an alteration of the morbidity experience with tuberculosis. The individual patient is saved countless hours of hospitalization and disability because of antibiotics, but these benefits do not accrue to the overall prevalence and incidence of the disease. Medicine is limited in its ability to influence the interaction between tuberculosis and human society, but can profoundly alter the natural history of the disease in the individual host.

Another example of medicine's limitations is the routine physical examination and specifically its recent modification, multiphasic health screening. Since the turn of the century, physicians and organized medicine have impressed upon the public the need for a routine check-up. Our underlying assumption has been set that the early detection of the disease, generally asymptomatic, will permit early intervention by the physician and thus either a cure is effected or there is significant alteration of the disease's natural history. This assumption is the basis of the annual physical exam, the American Cancer Society's "check-up and a check" program and the like. Unfortunately, the validity of this assumption remains unproven and in fact is generally contradicted by the available evidence.

The best known program providing multiphasic health screening is the

Kaiser-Permanente Health Plan in California. Ten years' experiences have yielded disappointing and at times contradictory results. Despite the huge investments in the screening program, an analysis comparing a screened and control population does not bear out any major benefits. Overall mortality in both was the same? Disability as assessed by days lost from work was slightly less in a single group of older men. This improvement, however, was counterbalanced by an increased hospitalization rate among women. Although there may be benefits in multiphasic screening, such benefits are not easily delineated or obvious.

Several other studies have confirmed these data from Kaiser-Permanete suggesting that at present the benefits of the routine physical examination and of multiphasic health screening are meager at best. These medical procedures, a fundamental part of medical practice, are severely limited in their ability to alter the natural history of disease sufficiently to effect morbidity and mortality statistics. These are but a few numerous instances in which the promises of medical science and health care are bankrupt. The limitations of medicine are indeed profound, but should not serve as an indictment of illness care.

Though the consequences of medical intervention into disease process is debatable, it is reasonable to suggest that the care given to the diseased individual is generally of high quality and in the balance adds to the quality of life such a person experiences. Put more bluntly, Robert Haggerty has written:

> "In sum, we can say that there is not much evidence that illness
> care (which is what medical care consists of) reduces mortality or
> morbidity very much."

What approach then should we have toward health maintenance if multiphasic screening and the routine physical examination are without major benefits? As some physicians have done, these procedures can be abandoned completely or the interval between doctor-patient contacts increased from the usual one year to two or more years. However, such an approach defaults in an area of clinical medicine where additional metrologies are becoming available and may prove successful. Furthermore, the physician should not ignore a responsibility for health that has been a part of the profession since Hippocrates. In fact, the potential influence of the physician as teacher on health is potentially more profound than that of the physician as healer. Several lines of evidence suggest a physician as teacher role in the daily practice of medicine. A series of papers from the California State Department of Public Health explored the relationship of a number of personal health practices and mortality. Using an interview technique on a large sample of families in Alameda County, Belloc and associates were able to document seven health habits that influence mortality experience. Intuitively sound, these practices read like a page from a grammar school health pamphlet, yet have the confirmation of a sophisticated epidemiologic study. The personal health habits are as follows:

1. 7-8 hours of sleep each night
2. Regular meals, including breakfast
3. No between meal snacks
4. Normal weight
5. Daily, strenuous exercise
6. No smoking
7. Moderate alcohol use

The effects of these practices are cumulative; that is, the more habits a person practices, the better is her mortality experience. For each age and sex group, mortality rates can be easily determined.

Evidence corroborative of the influence such habits have on health is certainly available for tobacco and alcohol. Perhaps the most dramatic data is that demonstrating significant differences in mortality between Utah, substantially Mormon with proscriptions for alcohol and tobacco, and Nevada. Emphysema, lung cancer, bronchitis, and heart disease are definitely linked to tobacco use. The impact of that causal link is so strong that Thomas McKeown, a renowned British epidemiologist, has started:

> "In developed countries, prevention of smoking, in particular, is the most powerful measure available, or likely to become available, for the protection of health. In terms of his expectation of life, a mature smoker would probably do better giving up cigarettes and giving up doctors than be retailing both."

Finally, there are major categories of mortality potentially affected by the physician teacher. These include an awareness of the magnitude of automobile related deaths, suicide, and known risk factors important to the genesis of atherosclerotic and hypertensive heart disease, besides those related to cigarette smoking. These factors include blood pressure, cholesterol, weight, and possibly diet.

Taken together there are at least seven health habits and a number of additional risk factors that are crucial to the development of the morbid and mortal events which account for the majority of all causes of death in all age groups. It is the purpose of this proposal to suggest a replacement for the annual physical check-up based upon (1) existing data about health, and (2) the concept of the physician as teacher. Rather than abandon the superficially healthy individual to fantasies about the integrity of her body, it is proposed that the physician help identify risk factors and poor health habits, and then seek to modify behavior or alter risk factors through the Promotive Health Assessment.

II. PROMOTIVE HEALTH ASSESSMENT

This program is based upon the information outlined in the Introduction and the desire to provide individual participant with a positive, active approach to health. After the identification of personal risk factors and health habits, educational efforts are concentrated to alter these factors and habits through reinforcement of behavior modification. The organization structure for the PROMOTIVE HEALTH ASSESSMENT draws heavily upon that developed by Health Hazard Appraisal at Methodist Hospital in Indianapolis. Using the manual (Robbins and Hall, 1970) How to Practice Prospective Medicine, an assessment of the probability of death in the subsequent ten years from specific causes can be defined for each person. As will be shown, the cumulative individual risk score is generated plus the possible reduction in risk provided certain prescriptions are followed.

In addition, Belloc's previously mentioned work from California provides a slightly different, though additive, theoretic framework. By identifying various health habits, a different (though undoubtedly comparable) risk index is defined. Behavior modification can then be directed toward behavioral changes in the areas of these habits. These two programs are here combined into an active approach to health and health maintenance wherein the physician-teacher participates with the individual in defining goals and in pursuing those goals in an individual educational program.

This particular plan is designed to determine the feasibility of and active promotive approach to health. No attempt will be made to show changes in morbidity or mortality statistics in what is of necessity an uncontrolled trial. An outline of this approach along with samples of the suggested forms follows. Appendix II contains the suggested forms completed on a fictitious patient.

A. Goals: This initial program is designed (1) to develop and market the PROMOTIVE HEALTH ASSESSMENT and (2) to develop the specific modes of intervention for motivating behavioral changes whether through health education classes, individual instruction, or self-instructional tools. In general such a program must be viewed as a project to determine the feasibility of these ideas.

B. Outcomes: Although the long range outcome measures will certainly have to be a change in morbidity and mortality statistics, the demonstration of successful behavioral changes during the developmental stages of this program must be taken as a sufficient outcome. A careful documentation of changes in morbidity and mortality experience will require a major controlled, clinical trial which is beyond the scope and intent of this proposal.

C. Administration: The Medical Director will be responsible for the coordination of the PROMOTIVE HEALTH ASSESSMENT program. Included here is the development of specific aspects of the program, periodic reporting, accounting, and evaluation.

D. Sites: The PROMOTIVE HEALTH ASSESSMENT program will be available in all three centers. Participation by local staff will depend upon acceptance of the basic plan after full development at the Chapel Hill-Carrboro facility.

E. Eligibility: All persons within the defined catchment areas of OCCHS, between 18 and 60 years old are eligible. The presence of chronic disease status does not alter eligibility, since the program is more broadly based than chronic disease therapy. Registration will be limited to new patients if response is greater than available resources.

F. <u>Participation:</u> Each individual within the program will be made aware of the PROMOTIVE HEALTH ASSESSMENT, consisting of two visits (see below). Participation in this or other aspects the program is completely voluntary.

G. <u>Costs:</u> Partial fee schedules are appended (Section IV). *Because of the time necessary to establish individual profiles and develop an individual PROSPECTIVE HEALTH PLAN, charges are slightly greater than the currently available routine history, physical, and laboratory fee, the unit charge (one year) for a PROSPECTIVE HEALTH PLAN will depending upon the complexity of the services offered.

*Available on request

A minimum charge of $10 is suggested for the initial assessment to cover extensive costs. Thereafter, fees are arranged according to the usual sliding schedule.

H. <u>Staffing:</u> Existing personnel will be utilized without interfering with their usual activities. Each provider will be responsible for the development of an individual PROSPECTIVE HEALTH PLAN from a list of available programs. Each provider is responsible for coordination of the PROSEPECTICE HEALTH PLAN with the Health Educator.

Additional secretarial support will be added as necessary

I. <u>Health Educator:</u> This person shall be responsible for the development of a number of educational programs designed to motivate specific behavioral change. In addition, PROMOTIVE HEALTH ASSESSMENT and HEALTH HABIT RISK charts (Appendix I, II)* are the responsibility of this person. These charts, along with other packaging materials, are given to the provider several days before the PROSPECTIVE HEALTH PLAN development visit.

J. <u>Initial Assessment:</u> When a person requests to join the PROMOTIVE HEALTH ASSESSMENT program, two appointments for an initial assessment are set up within two weeks of each other. A "history" form and a <u>Health Habits Appraisal</u> questionnaire are sent at least 2-3 weeks prior to the initial assessment.

> These forms appear in the Appendix I
>
> The first visit is for review of the history and performance of a physical examination and laboratory tests. In addition, a pamphlet explaining the various programs available to the individual is provided.

K. <u>Promotive Health Assessment:</u> At this second visit, copies of the PROMOTIVE HEALTH ASSESSMENT chart (appendix I and II) and HEALTH HABITS RISK chart are given to the patient. These charts are fully explained and an individual PROSPECTIVE HEALTH PLAN (Appendix I) developed that includes regular contact with the provider. A PROMOTIVE HEALTH RECORD. (Appendix I) is placed in the chart for following behavioral changes. Chronic disease maintenance is recorded as usual. Specific follow up testing is outline for each part of the program.

CONTINUING EDUCATION LOG

Provider Name: _____

CATEGORY I: TOPIC	DATE	NUMBER OF HOURS

Figure 7: Continuing Education Log

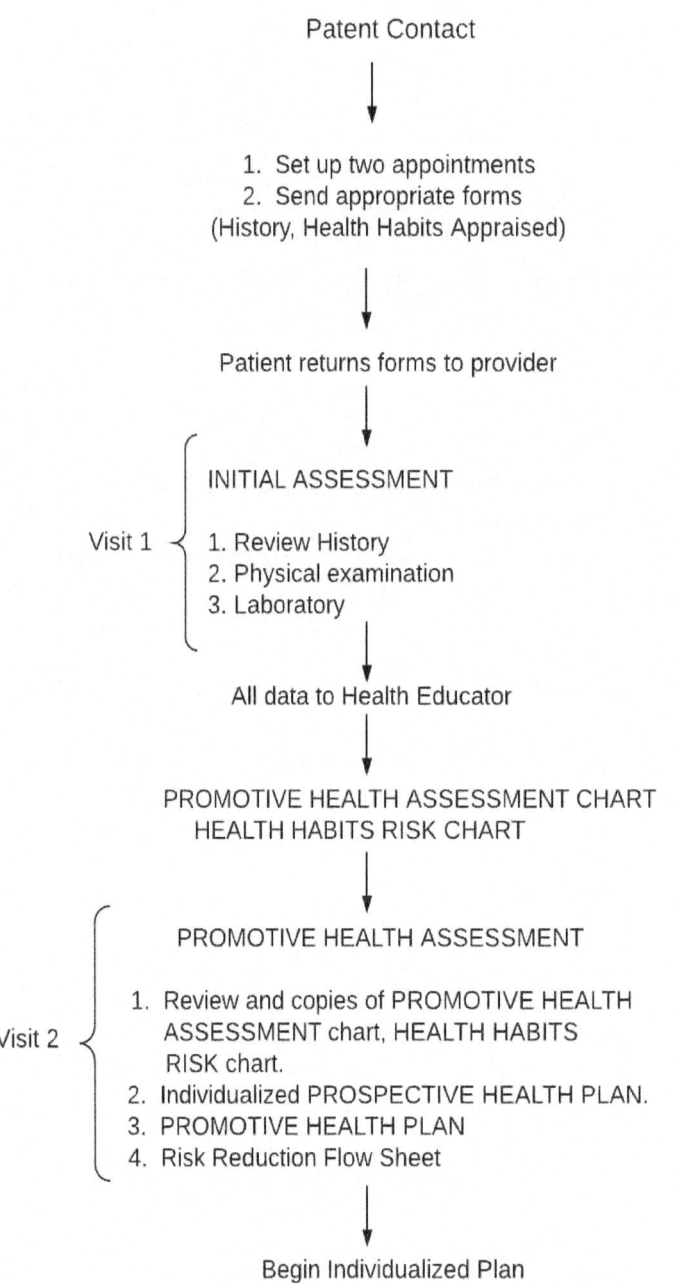

FLOW DIAGRAM
OF
PROMOTIVE HEALTH ASSESSMENT PROGRAM

Patent Contact

1. Set up two appointments
2. Send appropriate forms
(History, Health Habits Appraised)

Patient returns forms to provider

Visit 1

INITIAL ASSESSMENT

1. Review History
2. Physical examination
3. Laboratory

All data to Health Educator

PROMOTIVE HEALTH ASSESSMENT CHART
HEALTH HABITS RISK CHART

Visit 2

PROMOTIVE HEALTH ASSESSMENT

1. Review and copies of PROMOTIVE HEALTH
   ASSESSMENT chart, HEALTH HABITS
   RISK chart.
2. Individualized PROSPECTIVE HEALTH PLAN.
3. PROMOTIVE HEALTH PLAN
4. Risk Reduction Flow Sheet

Begin Individualized Plan

Figure 8: Flow Diagram of Piedmont Health Assessment Program

III. Possible Behavioral Interventions

1. Health Habits Groups: Group classes meeting on a regular basis to discuss various health habits for which the program does not provide an active approach. This would include much habits as automobile safety, home safety, sleep habits and stress. The focus of these classes would be toward methods available to modifying inadequate habits. Such classes could be given as a unit program over a several month period and refresher classes could be made available to those wanting additional instruction or motivation. These Health Habit Groups will be developed by the Health Educator and must be tailored to the specific needs of the different cultural and ethnic groups in the community.

2. Weight Control: Classes in the model of Weight Watchers International to motivate behavior changes vis-à-vis eating habits. Contracting with Weight Watchers International is presently under consideration. Individual counseling with the staff nutritionist is also available.

3. Dietary change: Classes and individualized counseling aimed at reducing intake of cholesterol, refined carbohydrates, saturated fat by altering dietary habits. Pertinent feedback can be developed including changes in weight and various biochemical parameters. Other diets can also be made available including vegetarian and high bulk.

4. Smoking: Efforts directed at stopping cigarette smoking must include all available modalities of behavior modification. Each of these avenues from group therapy to individualized psychotherapy will be will be explored. Additional motivating feedback may include intermittent pulmonary function testing to demonstrate resolution of pulmonary disorder.

5. Exercise: A jogging track in the immediate vicinity of each center is under current examination. On a regular basis this course could be walked or

jogged under supervision. The determination of vital signs before or after this exercise could serve as motivating feedback. Stress electrocardiography may be employed to assess underlying clinically significant coronary artery disease in men over 45 years of age and in women over 50 years of age. Other exercise programs including a contractual arrangement with a local health spa is currently under exploration.

6. Other programs: Additional modalities of behavioral motivation will be explored in an effort to expand the available programs. These modalities may include

14. Additional Program Services

Several pertinent areas were the subject of limited discussions and will require further inquiry later. These areas are included briefly here for future references and consideration.

a. County Health Department: Duplicate services are offered by OCCHS and the County Health Department, including immunization, screening, and well child clinics. Since both organizations are publicly funded ,it seems appropriate to begin considerations of coordinating some of these services so both institutions remain viable. Generally this means determining the extent of duplication coupled with reasonable efforts at a loose consolidation. This process can mean a more efficient utilization of limited resources for more people in the area. Preliminary discussions with Health Department Officials have started.

b. Extension of Services: Other communities, in particular Efland, have expressed a desire for medical services from OCCHS. Although outside all existing catchment areas, ways of establishing mall, satellite units should be explored. These units should not necessarily provide daily services initially, but may be able to meet the needs with short office hours several times a week.

c. Information System: OCCHS has developed a sophisticated information system containing data from thousands of patient encounters. Limited quantities of this data are ever returned to the program except monthly volume tallies and patient lists. The information system is capable of much more immediate feedback to each center if small terminals were available. Immediate display of medication records, problem lists, laboratory data, and patient profile is easily obtainable with the present system. Possibilities for the daily use of the information system should be explored, particularly any threats to patient confidentiality.

d. Clinical Investigation: An additional use of the data currently available is the investigation of clinically relevant questions, specifically treatment questions peculiar to the program. Such issues include the numbers of patients with certain diseases (hypertension, heart failure) and on certain drugs, the cost of care in a neighborhood health center, etc. While clinical investigation is not the primary mission of the program, we must document our experience to learn about mistakes or see better ways of providing care. Furthermore, these experiences can be invaluable to other health programs.

e. Consumer Feedback: One of the best sources of information about the quality of care given in each center is the patient. Informal lines of communication exist through the Community Health Worker. More formal means of patient input should also be developed in order to provide a broader consensus about any number of issues. Suggestion boxes can be supplemented with questionnaires and telephone surveys that seek responses from patients about the specific issues relevant to care. Mechanisms for consumer feedback need to be explored.

f. Additional Professional Services: The comprehensive ideal of OCCHS has led to the provision of some rather unique services within the same organizations structure, particularly optometry. Patient acceptance has been good.

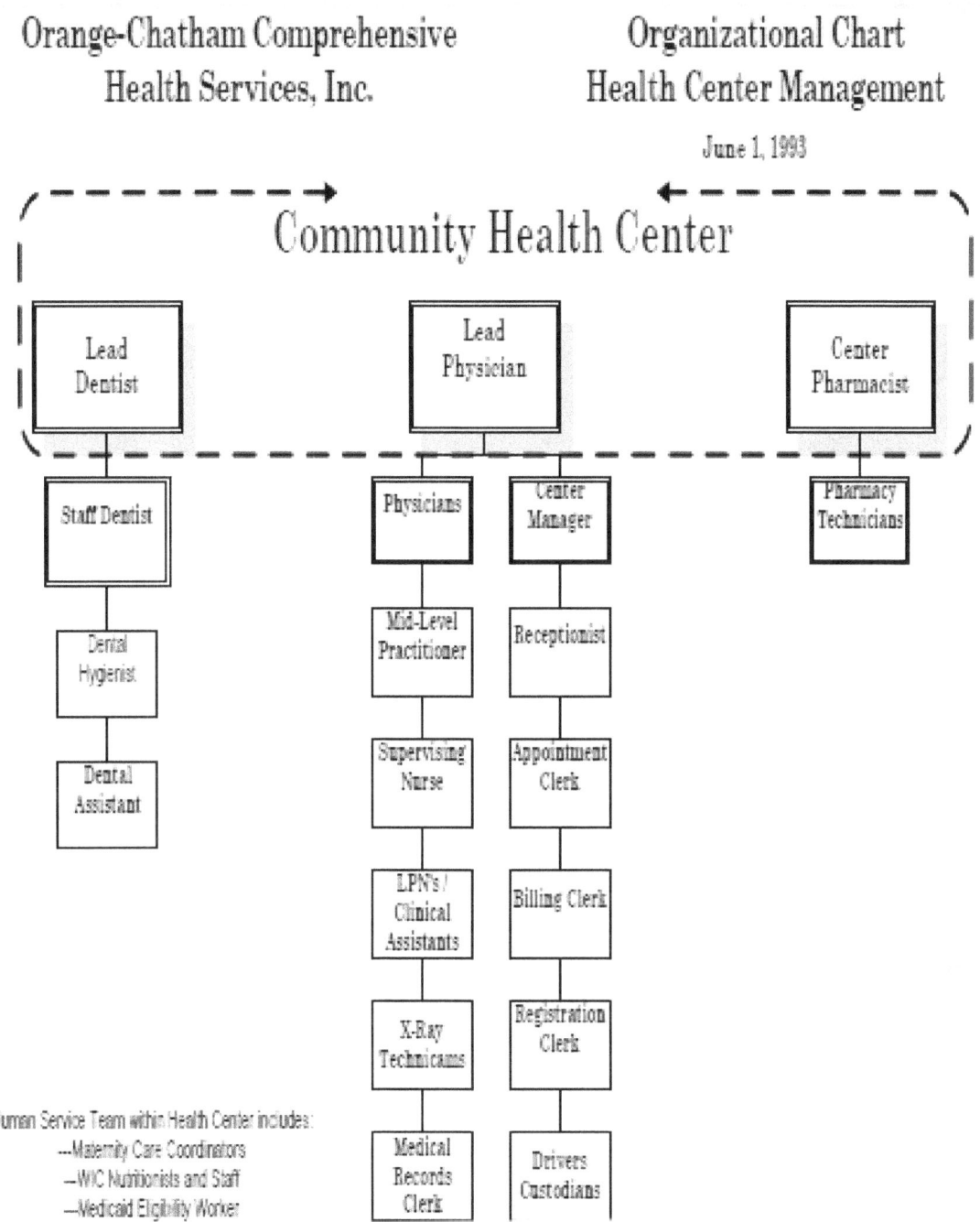

Figure 9: Comprehensive Organizational Chart

Orange-Chatham Comprehensive Health Services, Inc.
Promotive Health Assessment
History

A knowledge of your personal health history, including family history and habit patterns is most important in evaluating your health. Please complete this <u>confidential</u> form as accurately as possible. Approximate duties may be used. IF you need assistance please contact our office so your appointment can be scheduled slightly early. PLEASE USE DARK INK.

Please return this form in the enclosed envelope at least seven (7) days before your appointment. This time is necessary to fully evaluate the information you supply.
Thank you.

1. Name _____   2. Sex _____
        (Last)   (First)   (Initial)   4. Marital Status
                                                                                      a. Married ____
3. Address _____   b. Single_____
              (Number & Street)   (City & State)   c. Widowed___
                                                                              d. Separated__
                                                                              e. Divorced___

5. Phone Number _____

6. Age _____   7. Date of birth _____   8. Race
                              (Month) (Day) (Year)   a. White ____
                                                                              b. Negro ____
                                                                              c. Other ____

9. Place of birth _____
              (City & State or County)

FAST MEDICAL HISTORY. Please check each of the following you have had.

1. Old fashioned measles	22. Asthma	42. Lung operation
2. German (3 day) measles	23. Ulcer	43. Kidney operation
3. Mumps	24. Arthritis	44. Heart operation
4. Whooping cough	25. Gout	45. Breast operation
5. Scarlet fever	26. Treated for anemia	46. Bowel operation
6. Rheumatic fever	27. Hemophilia (bleeder)	47. Other operation(s)
7. Typhoid fever	28. Concussion	<u>Preventive Measures</u>
8. Pneumonia	29. Nervous breakdown	48. Tetanus shots
9. Tuberculosis	30. Convulsions	49. Diptheria shots
10. Chicken Pox	31. Emphysema	50. Typhoid shots
11. Gonorrhea	<u>Operations</u>	51. Whooping cough shots
12. Syphilis	32. Appendectomy	52. Polio shots
13. Kidney disease	33. Tonsillectomy	53. Oral polio vaccine
14. Kidney stone	34. Gall bladder removed	54. Measles vaccine
15. Hepatitis	35. Uterus removed	55. Smallpox vaccine
16. Jaundice	36. Tubers removed	56. TB skin test
17. Cancer	37. Ovaries removed	57. Last eye exam
18. Diabetes	38. Stomach operation	58. Pap smear
19. Heart trouble	39. Hernia repair	59. Chest x-ray
20. High blood pressure	40. Hemorrhoid surgery	60. Electrocardiogram
21. Hay fever	41. Prostate operations	

Name _____

61. Allergies: Please list any medication, cosmetic, or food allergies and describe reaction. (Such as: penicillin or eggs cause hives.) _____

_____

62. Do you have deformity which interferes with your daily activities? If so, what?

_____

63. I last saw a doctor _____Date_____ Reason _____

64. Hospitalization (except childbirth)

Year	Hospital & Location	How long?	Diagnosis & Treatment

65. Do you recall any other important past medical history? (List blood transfusions, other surgery, injuries, allergy treatments, special lab tests, etc. if applicable.)

_____

_____

_____

II. FAMILY HISTORY

Please list all relatives mentioned below by name				State of health (Please check)			Age now or at death	Please state chief or cause of death if known
				Cond	Poor	Deceased		
1. Father								
2. Mother								
3. Wife or husband								
List by name:	Brother	Sister	Son	Daughter				
4								
5.								
6.								
7.								
8.								
9.								
10.								
11.								
12.								
13.								

Figure 10: Promotive Health Assessment

APPENDIX 1

Jean Dowdy~Marjorie Land~Glenda Hargraves

Orange Chatham Comprehensive Health Services, Inc.

108 Roberson Street   Telephone 919-942-8741

Carrboro, North Carolina 27510

PROMOTIVE HEALTH ASSESSMENT

HEALTH HABITS

_____

(NAME)

DATE: _____

PERRSONAL HEALTH HABITS	ESTIMATED RISK	
	(Do not write in this space)	
	PREENT	REDUCED

Weight: _____

Height:_____

Do you smoke? Cigarettes-2 or more packs per day ____ Cigarettes-1½ packs per day ____ Cigarettes-1 pack per day ____ Cigarettes ½ pack per day ____ Cigarettes-less than ½ pack per day ____ Cigars or pipe-5 or more per day ____ Cigars or pipe-less than 5 per day ____		
Do you drink alcoholic beverages? Yes ____ No ____ If yes, how much do you drink: 2 or less drinks per week ____ 3 to 6 drinks per week ____ 7 to 24 drinks per week ____ 25 to 40 drinks per week ____ More than 40 drinks per week ____		
Please mark the one answer that best describes how much exercise you do, including your work. Climbing less than 5 flights of stairs or walking less than ½ mile 4 times per week, or other equal exercise. ____ Climbing 5 to 15 flights of stairs or walking ½ to 1½ miles 4 times per week, or other equal exercise. ____ Climbing 15 to 20 flights of stairs or walking 1 ½ to 2 miles 4 times per week, or other equal exercise._ Exercise greater than any of these. ____		

RSONAL HEALTH HABITS   ESTIMATED   RISK

(Do not write in this space)

	PREENT	REDUCED
Check the number of hours of sleep you get each night. Less than 6 hours per night ____ 6-7 hours per night ____ 7-8 hours per night ____ More than 8 hours per night ____		
Check the meals you regularly eat: Breakfast ____ Lunch ____ Dinner ____		
Do you regularly have a between meal snack? Yes ____ No ____ Please check the snacks you regularly have: Morning snack ____ Afternoon snack ____ Evening snack ____		

TOTAL RISK: _____

Health Educator

Orange Chatham Comprehensive Health Services, Inc.

108 Roberson Street   Telephone 919-942-8741

Carrboro, North Carolina 27510

HEALTH HABITS APPRAISAL

NAME:_____

	PRESENT RISK	REDUCED RISK
1 SLEEP		
2 MEALS		
3 SNACKS		
4 WEIGHT		
5 EXERCISE		
6 SMOKING		
7 DRINKING		
TOTAL		

Figure 4: Health Habits Appraisal

ABOUT THE AUTHORS

Jean Dowdy, currently retired is Registered Nurse, Family Nurse Practitioner and has a Bachelor of Art degree from North Carolina Agricultural State University. Dowdy was a faithful and dedicated FNP for Orange Chatham Comprehensive Health Services Inc. and Piedmont Health Services for 28 years, retiring on December 9, 2005.

Marjorie Land graduated from North Carolina Agricultural and Technical College (now North Carolina A&T State University) with a Bachelor of Science in Nursing. Land received her Family Nurse Practitioner from the Continuing Education Program at University of North Carolina at Chapel Hill in 1971.
Land worked at all of the three original centers: Prospect Hill, Haywood-Moncure and Chapel Hill. Land was assigned to the Chapel Hill Community Health Center.

Glenda Hargraves, retired Registered Nurse and Certified Family Nurse Practitioner, worked at the Orange Chatham Comprehensive Health Services, Inc./Piedmont Health Services for 27 years.

www.ingramcontent.com/pod-product-compliance
Lightning Source LLC
Chambersburg PA
CBHW080958020726
47505CB00009B/2252